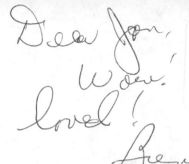

STRANGER TO SELF-HATRED

A Glimpse of Jesus

by

Brennan Manning T.O.R.

DIMENSION BOOKS
Denville, New Jersey

ACKNOWLEDGMENTS

The light of the Word, the vision of Albert Nolan O.P., Ernst Kasemann and Donald Gray, the spirit of the House of Affirmation, and the insights of many Christian writers, teachers and friends are so integral to this book that, except for a few personal experiences and reflections, its real author is the Body of Christ.

DEDICATION

To Roslyn whose compassion, vulnerability and obedience to the Word have revealed to me and others the human face of God.

ISBN 0-87193-183-4 Hardcover
ISBN 0-87193-156-7 Paperback

Published by Dimension Books, Inc.

Denville, New Jersey 07834

TABLE OF CONTENTS

FOREWORD

This little book pretends to be no more than the subtitle claims: a glimpse of Jesus. That is all I have. It is written for myself and anyone else who has been tyrannized by self-hatred. I envision a wide reading audience because self-hatred is the predominant spiritual problem that I have had to deal with in six years as a vagabond evangelist.

Unhealthy guilt, shame, remorse and self-hatred are no respecter of persons. Vague feelings of existential uneasiness before the Lord God transcend poverty and wealth, cultural and educational differences, distinctions between clergy and laity.

While *Stranger to Self-Hatred* is polemical in places, it never questions the integrity of the present leadership of the church of Jesus Christ or the pastoral concern of its theological enterprise. Blaming Rome is a jejune counterproductive defense mechanism for which I have neither the time nor the heart. The Catholic Church is the locus of my encounter with Jesus Christ. One of the several purposes within these pages is to contribute to the raising of community consciousness at the grass roots level. A fearless re-examination of ecclesiastical values, attitudes and practice is part of the ongoing task of aggiornamento initiated by the late Pope John XXIII.

The sweeping implications of the social dimension of the gospel, so vital for Christian renewal, are left largely untreated because of the limited scope of the subject. A glimpse is a glimpse and nothing more. And nothing less.

Perhaps what is decisive is not how much we see, but how much we have believed and followed Jesus of Nazareth, however sketchy the portrait, however partial the glimpse.

ONE

THE SCRIPT FOR SELF-HATRED

In Flannery O'Connor's short story, *The Turkey,*[1] the anti-hero and principal protagonist is a little boy named Ruller. He has a poor self-image because whatever he turns his hand to never seems to work. At night in bed he overhears his parents analyzing him. "Ruller's an unusual one," his father says. "Why does he always play by himself?" And his mother answers, "How am I to know?"

One day in the woods Ruller spots a wild and wounded turkey and sets off in hot pursuit. "Oh, if only I can catch it," he cries. He will catch it, even if he has to run it out of state. He sees himself triumphantly marching through the front door of his house with the turkey slung over his shoulder and the whole family screaming, "Look at Ruller with that wild turkey! Ruller, where did you get that turkey?"

"Oh, I caught it in the woods. Maybe you would like me to catch you one sometime."

But then the thought flashed across his mind, "God will probably make me chase that damn turkey all afternoon for nothing." Hmnn, shouldn't think that way about God though; yet that was the way he felt. If that was the way he felt, could he help it? He wondered if he were unusual.

Ruller finally captures the turkey when it rolls over dead from a previous gunshot wound. He hoists it on his shoulders and begins his messianic march back through the center of town. He remembered the things he had thought before he got the bird. They were pretty bad, he guessed. He figured God had stopped him before it was too late. He should be very thankful. "Thank you, God," he said. "Much obliged to you. This turkey must weigh ten pounds. You were mighty generous."

Maybe getting the turkey was a sign, he thought. Maybe God wanted him to be a preacher. He thought of Bing Crosby and Spencer Tracy. He entered town with the turkey slung over his shoulder. He wanted to do something for God but he didn't know what to do. If anybody was playing the accordion on the street today, he would give them his dime. It was the only dime he had but he would give it to them.

Two men approached and whistled at the turkey. They yelled at some other men on the corner to look. "How much do you think it weighs," they asked. "At least ten pounds," Ruller answered. "How long did you chase it?" "About an hour," said Ruller. "That's really amazing. You must be very tired." "No, but I have to go," Ruller replied, "I'm in a hurry." He could not wait to get home.

He began to wish he would see somebody begging. Suddenly he prayed, "Lord, send me a beggar. Send me one before I get home." God had put the turkey there. Surely God would send him a beggar. He knew for a fact God would send him one. God was interested in him because he was an unusual child. "Please, one right now" — and the minute he said it, an old beggar woman headed straight at him. His heart was stomping up and down in his chest. As they neared each other, he sprang at the woman shouting, "Here, here," thrust the dime into her hand and dashed on without looking back.

Slowly his heart calmed and he began to feel full of a new feeling — like being happy and embarrassed at the same time. Maybe, he thought, he would give all his money to her. He felt as if the ground did not need to be under him any longer.

Ruller noticed a group of country boys shuffling behind him. He turned round and asked generously, "Y'all wanna see this turkey?" They stared at him. "Where did ya git that turkey?"

"I found it in the woods. I chased it dead. See, it's been shot under the wing."

"Lemme see it," one boy said. Ruller handed him the turkey. The turkey's head flew into his face as the country boy slung it up in the air and over his own shoulder and turned. The others turned with him and sauntered away.

They were a quarter-mile away before Ruller moved. Finally he realized that he couldn't even see them anymore, they were so far away. Then he turned toward home almost creeping. He walked for a bit and then, noticing it was dark, suddenly began to run. And Flannery O'Connor's exquisite tale ends with the words: "He ran faster and faster, and as he turned up the road to his house, his heart was running as fast as his legs and he was certain that Something Awful was tearing behind him with its arms rigid and its fingers ready to clutch."

The story hardly needs any commentary for in little Ruller many of us Christians stand revealed, naked, exposed. Our God is One who benevolently gives turkeys and then capriciously takes them away. When He gives them, they are a sign of his interest, favor and good pleasure with us. We feel comfortably close to God and are spurred to the heights of generosity. When He takes them away, it is a sign of his displeasure, rejection and vengeance. We feel cast off by God. He is fickle, unpredictable, whimsical. He only builds us up to let us down. He relentlessly remembers our past sins and vindictively retaliates by snatching the turkeys of good health, wealth, inner peace, empire, success and joy.

The script for self-hatred starts here. As Blaise Pascal wrote, "God made man in his own image and man returned the compliment." The mechanism of projection is a process of unwittingly ascribing to God our own attitudes and feelings as an unconscious defense of our own inadequacy or guilt. "Indeed, much of the distortion that does enter into our notion of God is introduced in each person's primitive period — his youth.

From his parents a child learns of a God who strongly disapproves of disobedience, and hitting one's brothers and sisters and telling lies. The youngster goes to school and finds that God also shares the many concerns, sometimes fussy ones, of his teachers. At church, the god of the parish priest has a somewhat different set of priorities. Emphasis is laid upon Mass and Confession and Communion, and though it is beyond his own horizon of interest, the child is aware that God often makes recurring and emphatic fiscal demands upon the parishioners. When he reaches the age for high school, he finds that God's own interests have expanded: he is obsessed with sex and drinking and drugs. After he emerges from his youth altogether he discovers — sometimes with resentment — that God has been used as a sanction for all those who were responsible for his discipline. When he used to cavort a bit mischievously at home, his mother might reach the end of her patience and persuasiveness and threaten, 'When Daddy comes home, he'll take care of you.' But if Mommy and Daddy are both at their wits' end, there is always the eternal spanking to which they can and do allude. God is thus unwittingly associated with fear."[2]

The Christian world, which incessantly projects its own god fashioned after its own image, pays a heavy price in anxiety, scrupulosity and a vague sense of existential guilt. "These feelings come from within ourselves and are projected outward into the mind of God. We may find that we punish ourselves mercilessly for real or imagined sins, and even then we will not forgive ourselves . . . Fortunately Christ has revealed the real God to us in unmistakably human form, exposed projection for the idolatry that it is, and given us the way to become free from it. It takes a profound conversion to accept the belief that God is tender and loves us just as we are, not in spite of our sins and faults, but with them. God does not condone or sanction evil, but he does not withhold his love because there is evil in us. The key to this understanding is the way we feel about ourselves. We cannot even stand or accept love from another human being when we do not love ourselves, much less believe or accept that God could possibly love us."[3]

Whether envisioned as an omnipotent thug stealing our inner peace or as Something Awful tearing behind us, these distortions and caricatures of the God revealed by and in Jesus engender fear, anger, self-hatred and a nagging sense of insecurity about ever being in right relationship with God. The past six years of tramping about the country as an evangelist and dealing daily with street people have made it luminously clear that religious projection is remarkably widespread and that self-hatred is rampant.

Perfectionism

The perfectionist in the spiritual life is locked into the saint-or-sinner syndrome, tyrannized by an all or nothing mentality. Informed by his spiritual director that he is probably in the sixth mansion of St. Teresa's *Interior Castle,* he grieves that he is not in the seventh. He vows to try harder and search the library to see if George Maloney or Richard Woods has written anything new on mysticism. Compulsive and constant moralistic self-evaluation preclude the serene acceptance of his poverty before God. "I hope it is clear that feelings of guilt, accompanied by anxiety, fear and restlessness, arise from deep within ourselves and are not an accurate gauge of the state of our souls before God. We cannot assume that he feels about us the way we feel about ourselves, unless we love ourselves intensely and freely."[4]

The perfectionist interprets weakness as mediocrity and inconsistency as a loss of nerve. The desire for perfection transcends the desire for God. The example of Mother Teresa, Daniel Berrigan or Carlo Carretto is not an inspiration but a reproach. The painful consciousness of having sold out for small comforts that now seem indispensable and the small compromises growing more numerous that now seem irreversible are a source of deep distress. A compassionate attitude of self-acceptance is simply unacceptable. The notion that sin and grace can co-exist simultaneously in the same person, that imperfection and inspiration are not mutually exclusive is a maudlin concession valid only for those not striving for spiritual excellence. Yet St. Paul writes, "though the will to do what is good is in me, the performance is not, with the result that instead of doing the good things I want to do, I carry out the sinful things I do not want."[5] Father Bernard Bush S. J. notes, "It has never been expressed so succinctly. St. Paul can even find the hand of God and a response of praise in the contemplation of his own sinfulness."[6]

But because the perfectionist measures his personal worth before God in terms of the acquisition of virtue and the elimination of vice, because his vision is a triumphal and uninterrupted forced march along the purgative and illuminative trails to the unitive bivouac, the outcome is an unrealistically negative self-image. There is a conspicuous absence of peace and joy. The yawning gulf between the ideal self and the real self makes an attitude of gratitude implausible and the likelihood of wide mood swings highly probable.

"Perfectionist individuals, we find, are likely to respond to the perception of failure or inadequacy with a precipitous loss in self-esteem that can trigger episodes of severe depression and anxiety."[7] The compulsive drive for spiritual perfection is not born of the Spirit of God and only adds another scenario to the script for self-hatred.

Moralism

The habit of moralizing spoils religion. Personal responsibility to an inviolable moral code replaces personal response to God's loving call. Moralism and its stepchild legalism reduce the love story of God for his people to the observance of burdensome duties and oppressive laws. The legalist deformation of religion concerns itself with shadow not substance. At the funeral home, a well-intentioned friend eulogizes the deceased: "John was a wonderful Catholic. He never missed Sunday Mass, was married only once, and of course he never told a dirty joke." Here the criterion for holiness and the ultimate sign of religious surrender is observance of the Law. The Pharisees did as much!

"Legalism creates a mask of conformity which makes the believer holy in his eyes and thus prevents him from coming to self-knowledge. Legalistic religion stresses will-power, and it is this very stress on personal effort that makes the legalist unaware of his real feelings, of his own brokenness, and hence of his need for redemption . . . He tends to despise the men and women who are not as observant as he. Thus he elevates himself above the sinner, the outsider, the non-conformist. Because of this self-elevation, this reliance on self, coupled with lack of self-knowledge, the legalist renders himself incapable of receiving divine grace; he does not live by faith."[8]

The Moral Majority in the United States represents a pathetic caricature of biblical religion. The face of a compassionate God is completely obscured. The best principles of the Christian heritage are ignored in favor of a hard moralism wherein the demonic dimension overshadows the loving dimension of the Gospel. Their legalistic formulations attempt to dominate American moral perspective, limit moral options and even replace moral insight. The God of the Moral Majority is an exacting lawgiver, a stern taskmaster; the Good News of Jesus Christ takes on a cutting fanatical edge; the force of the Gospel message is distorted into something basically threatening.

"The smug Christian finds a perverse vindictive satisfaction in anticipating the fate of those whom he considers his own enemies and God's as well. Thus certain elements present in the New Testament can be isolated and inflated to a point where they distort the whole central significance of the New Testament and pervert the whole character of the Christian life. Just as Christian belief has its heresies of thought, so too Christian ethics has its heresies of attitude and behavior. To accept the Gospel in faith is to respect its emphases and preserve its balance."[9]

Let the Christian community cry out in anger against these lying slogans that pile up with impunity! Rev. Jerry Falwell decries the horror of pornography, yet justifies the proliferation of nuclear weapons and the use of the atomic bomb. It sounds rational: a bit of genocide and world-wide devastation is a minor evangelical matter compared to getting the smut-peddlers off the street. What a travesty of the Gospel and what bad press for authentic religion! "The creator whom one can play off against the creature is a false god," writes Ernst Kasemann, "and false gods rob even pious people of their humanity, as is shown times without number in the church's history."[10]

Unfortunately religion readily lends itself to legalistic misunderstanding. The reliance on ceremonies and the observance of commandments too easily leads to a false trust in the external elements of religion and creates a mystique of spiritual superiority. Does the neutral onlooker identify a Catholic Christian by his pious practices and cultic regularity or by the loving quality of his everyday presence in

the workaday world? "The greatest millstone around
the neck of organized religion is not its authority
figures but the too facile acceptance on the part of
leaders and members that ritual and cult can substitute for personal commitment and the sacrifice of
one's life."[11]

From another perspective legalism attempts to
determine every moral choice on the basis of existing
regulations. Law thus tends to become an end in
itself, rather than a means to an end. The result is the
frustration of the very reason that brought the law
into being. Jesus resolutely insisted that law was the
expression of the love of God and neighbor and that
piety that stands in the way of love stands in the way
of God himself. "Such freedom challenged the Jewish
system. Yet Jesus says he has not come to destroy the
law but to fulfill it. What he offers is not a new law
but a new attitude toward law, an attitude based on
being human and loving."[12]

Furthermore, Jesus shattered the legalistic notion
of reward for moral performance and any self-
righteous expectation of a higher rung on the
heavenly ladder. The bartering mentality of "I've
done this, therefore you owe me that," is brushed
aside in the scandalous parable of the Laborers in the
Vineyard (Mt. 20:1-16) Salvation cannot be earned or
merited but only humbly and gratefully received as a
loving gift from the Father's hand. (Somewhere in
Flannery O'Connor's works there is an outrageous
image of the Last Judgment where the sinners and
tax-collectors are dancing into the Kingdom while the
'just' are in the background having their virtue burnt
out of them!). All is gift and gracious clemency as the
parable of the Prodigal vividly reminds us. "To
demand a higher reward for achievement (because,

for instance, one lives a celibate life for the kingdom's sake) and to become angry (because the younger brother who likewise has offered his life for the cause of the kingdom, gets married) is by this parable held up to ridicule as an attitude directly militating against the praxis of the kingdom of God. Whatever the material verdict on the case, both celibacy as being a claim upon a higher reward and being resentful of the younger brother are attitudes alien to the orthopraxis of the kingdom of God."[13]

To me the excommunication of Father Francis MacNutt, the late Walter Imbiorski, and other married priests denied the rescript of laicization is a tragedy, a Christian scandal and blatant testimony to the perverse perduring power of moralism/legalism in the contemporary Church. I firmly believe that if we courageously sought a *consensus fidelium,* the Spirit of God who speaks through the Body of Christ would verify this conviction.

Sadly, legalistic religion remains a dimension of the Christian life and spawns a curious species of self-hatred. There are no statistics to help ascertain how many Christians are kept away from the Church and deprived of an active sacramental life by the frightening fear-inducing antics of the legalistic mentality. But a mother of five children who came to me recently for counseling speaks for them all: "I don't come to Church anymore because we practice birth control. I would feel like a hypocrite."

The Church in all its structures and sacramentality should contribute to the resolution of self-hatred rather than write another chapter for the script. "For it believes in a Father before whom there can be no disgrace. He can have no contempt for us, since our infamies are nothing in his eyes. Yet churchmen have ever been tempted to use people's native shame to maneuver into a position of advantage with them. The Lord whose cherishing should be our greatest source of peace is again and again disfigured by morbid preachers who prefer a god of wrath."[14]

Unhealthy Guilt

Healthy guilt adds not a single paragraph to the script for self-hatred. The conviction of personal sinfulness leads to realistic confrontation, ruthless honesty and self-knowledge; it stimulates compunction, contrition, the desire for reconciliation and inner peace. As in any lovers' quarrel, the making-up not only absolves the past but brings a new depth of trust and security to the relationship. There is more power in sharing our weaknesses than our strengths. The forgiveness of God is gratuitous and unconditional liberation from the domination of guilt. He overlooks our past, takes away present or future consequences of past transgressions and causes us to cry out, "O felix culpa!" The sinful and repentant prodigal son experienced an intimacy and joy with his Father in his brokenness that his sinless self-righteous brother would never know.

Perhaps the most powerful charism of the fellowship of Alcoholics Anonymous is to lead its members to full ownership of their brokenness, to publicly acknowledge their failure to accept responsibility for their humanness. When called upon to speak, the alcoholic begins, "My name is Brennan. I am an alcoholic." There is no hedging, fudging, minimizing, rationalizing or justifying of my sickness. Only a candid admission that once I take that first drink

I can neither guarantee my behavior nor predict when I will stop, that I am a victim of an allergy of the body coupled with an obsession of the mind, that I am powerless over alcohol and that my life has become unmanageable. The grace of AA is to open my eyes to myself, to give me healthy guilt, to tell me things that my best friends should be telling me but won't. It invites me to confess my weakness at the very moment I am turning away from it. It urges no embarrassment on me. The drunkologue is a narrative of my ersatz behavior while under the influence and temporary insanity of alcohol. Wittingly or unwittingly, the empathy, compassion and unconditional acceptance of the members give me a glimpse of the unflinching love of the Abba of Jesus who cannot despise.

These words of the German theologian Walter Kasper could have been written with the AA brotherhood in mind: "The all-surpassing love of God makes itself felt in the acceptance of human beings by each other, in the dismantling of prejudices and social barriers, in new unrestricted communication among men, in brotherly warmth and the sharing of sadness and joy."[15]

The sacramental and non-sacramental sharing of healthy guilt is purgative and cathartic, introduces objectivity, banishes self-hatred and becomes the occasion of gracious encounter with the merciful love of the redeeming God.

However let us suppose that after seven years of marriage a couple has their first serious spat. Tempers flare, hostile words are exchanged and in a fit of anger the husband slaps his wife, storms out the door and retreats to the corner saloon. He orders a whiskey and beer chaser and begins to reflect: "I love that woman. She is the warm center of my world. Without her my life loses meaning, direction and purpose. And I just blew it. I hurt the one person who means more to me than anyone else. Hell, what am I doing sitting here? Every minute wasted on this barstool could be spent loving her." He leaves his drink untouched, dashes down the street, up the stairs and with a heart crushed with sorrow falls into his wife's arms.

Healthy guilt is other-centered, arouses compunction and the desire for reconciliation and calls a man into the fulness of manhood by staring in the face defiantly and without embarrassment the gods of pride, arrogance, self-righteousness and self-pity. "Learn from me," the Master said, "for I am gentle and humble in heart."

On the other hand, suppose the husband entrenched on the barstool ruminates: "I claim to be a Christian husband and I just humiliated, insulted, vilified and physically abused my wife. I lector at Mass on Sunday and people think I'm a model Catholic. I'm a damn hypocrite and a pious fraud." He orders a double from the bartender. "What have all these years of church-going done for me? Not an ounce of patience, not a whit of understanding. I'm a sewer, I'm a sewer, a great big cesspool . . . " The pity-party and the drinking continue until he has neither of his oars in the water and his drunken little rowboat is towed home by other sympathetic sailors in the pub.

Unhealthy guilt is self-centered, stirs our emotions to churning in self-destructive ways, leads to depression and despair, closes us in upon ourselves and pre-empts the presence of a compassionate God. "The language of unhealthy guilt is one of harshness. It is demanding, abusive, criticizing, rejecting, finding fault with, accusing, blaming, condemning, reproaching and scolding. It is one of impatience and chastisement. Persons are shocked and horrified because they failed. Unhealthy guilt becomes bigger than life. It is seen as the beginning and the end. In unhealthy guilt, the image of the childhood story "Chicken Little" comes to mind. Guilt becomes the experience in which people feel that the sky is falling."[16]

When God introduces creative tension into our lives by calling us to break camp, abandon the security and comfort of the status quo, and embark in perilous freedom on a new exodus, our insecurity and procrastination may focus only and the darker implications of the challenge and plunge us anew into unhealthy guilt. Stubbornly to stand still when the Lord is clearly challenging us to growth is hard-heartedness, infidelity and a dangerous lack of trust. But to start trekking across the desert impulsively without the guidance of the cloud and the fire is reckless folly. When God's call is not clarified and the inner voice remains indistinct, our restlessness and interior disquiet may be signalling a new exodus into greater openness, vulnerability and compassion, a deeper purity of heart, a transformed mind and spirit. The landscape of the American Church is littered with burntout bodies and abortive ministries born of unhealthy guilt and fear of resisting God's Will.

Who will acquit us from guilt? Who will free us from the bondage of projectionism, perfectionism and moralism? Who will re-write the script? Thanks be to God for Jesus Christ our Lord!

Footnotes

¹ *The Short Stories of Flannery O'Connor.* Farrar, Strauss and Giroux, N.Y., N.Y. 1971. p. 42-54.

² *Philemon's Problem.* James T. Burtchaell, C.S.C. ACTA Foundation, Chicago, Il., 1973. p. 18.

³ *Coping — First Boston Psychotheological Symposium.* Affirmation Books, Whitinsville, MA, 1976. The excerpt is from an inspired essay, "Coping With God," by Bernard Bush S.J.

⁴ Ibid.

⁵ *Romans* 7:18-19. (JB)

⁶ Bush, Ibid.

⁷ *Psychology Today:* The Perfectionist's Script for Self-Defeat. David S. Burns. N.Y., N.Y. November, 1980, p. 34.

⁸ *Religion and Alienation; A Theological Reading of Sociology.* Gregory Baum. Paulist Press, N.Y., N.Y. 1975. p. 68.

⁹ *Newness of Life: A Modern Introduction to Catholic Ethics.* James Gaffney, Paulist Press, N.Y., N.Y. 1979. p. 89.

¹⁰ *Jesus Means Freedom.* Ernst Kasemann. Fortress Press, Philadelphia, Pa., 1969. p. 26.

¹¹ *I Am What I Do: Contemplation and Human Experience.* Barbara Doherty. Thomas More Press, Chicago, Il. 1981. p. 12.

¹² *Jesus, Lord and Christ.* John F. O'Grady. Paulist Press, N.Y., N.Y. 1973. p. 14.

¹³ *Jesus: An Experiment in Christology,* Edward Schillebeeckx. Seabury Press, N.Y., N.Y. 1979. p. 165.

¹⁴ Burtchaell. Ibid.

¹⁵ *Jesus the Christ.* Walter Kasper. Paulist Press, N.Y., N.Y. 1977. p. 86.

¹⁶ *Guilt — Fifth Psychotheological Symposium.* Affirmation Books, Whitinsville, MA., 1980. Quoted from the essay, "Guilty: For Betraying Who I Am", by Vincent Bilotta III. p. 107.

TWO

JESUS — STRANGER TO SELF-HATRED

The only valid reason I can think of for living is Jesus Christ.

Who is this Jesus who is a magnetic field for so many Christians and a stumbling block for countless others?

The Council of Chalcedon in 451 A.D. answered that he is the incarnation of the Second Person of the Blessed Trinity. Contemporary theology offers varied answers: Jesus is the man for others, the ethical liberator, personal savior, the human face of God. Artists and poets speak of Jesus the clown, the mythological man and the superstar.

"To the question: 'But who do you say that I am?' many Church people and theologians are well able to say what answer has been given by Mark and Luke, Augustine, Thomas and Bellarmine, Luther and Calvin, Barth or Bultmann, Pannenberg or Rahner. *It is their own answer that we do not hear.* (Italics mine) Other people cannot answer on our behalf or supply us with the appropriate images, concepts and expressions: that would not be our response to the parable that is the life of Jesus . . . Each of us is confronted with this 'lived parable'. How do we interpret him? No one else — neither the historical disciplines nor theology nor even the first Christians nor yet the Church's magisterium — can answer that question for us. As we hear the parable the question is put to us: whether we will bet our life on it."[1]

The challenge, so keenly put in the New Testament: "Who do you say that I am?" is addressed to each of us. Who is the Jesus of your own interiority? Describe the Christ that you have personally encountered on the grounds of your own self.

Only a superficial stereotyped answer can be forthcoming if we have not developed a personal relationship with Jesus. We can only repeat and reproduce pious turns of speech that others have spoken or wave a catechism under children's noses if we have not gained some partial insight, some small perception of the inexhaustible richness of the mystery who is Jesus Christ.

Elsewhere[2] I wrote, "the Gospel of John is not the gospel of the Kingdom but the Gospel of Jesus himself. It is impossible to exaggerate the central position of Jesus in the fourth gospel. Central not merely because he is principal protagonist and teacher, but insofar as he illumines every page of it . . . The reader is, as it were, blinded by the brilliance of his image and comes away like a man who has looked long at the sun — unable to see anything but its light." John is concerned with one thing only — the person of Jesus. Do we know him? Everything else fades into twilight and darkness; it becomes irrelevant and is shunted aside. A person's life has meaning only inasmuch as he has prophetic truck with the Nazarene. "There is only Christ: he is everything." (Col. 3:11)

One way I have come to know Jesus is by empathetic identification with marginal characters in the gospel narrative. My background as a sergeant in the Marine Corps lends to relatively easy rapport with the centurion. Remember the day that Jesus healed his servant? The military man falls down and says, "Sir, I am not worthy to have you enter under my roof. Just give an order and my boy will get better." (Mt. 8:8) But the most revealing line in that story, according to Matthew, is that "Jesus was astonished." He spun round and cried out, "I tell you solemnly, nowhere in Israel have I found faith like this." At last, Jesus is saying, finally there is someone who understands me and what I want to be for my people — a Savior of boundless compassion, unbearable forgiveness, infinite patience and healing love. Will the rest of you let me be who I am and stop imposing your small, silly and self-styled ideas of who you think I ought to be!"

Small wonder that Fr. Richard Rohr would say, "The old Baltimore catechism isn't wrong, just inadequate. When it says, 'Man is made to know, love and serve God,' it should read, man is made to know how God longs to love and serve him." Jesus remains Lord by serving us. "According to Luke 12:37, in fact, the world's Judge on the last day will once more gird himself as a slave."[2] It will go well with those servants whom the master finds wide-awake on his return. I tell you, he will put on an apron, seat them at table, and proceed to wait on them. Christian freedom is the joyful acceptance of this unprecedented and scandalous reversal of the world's values. In sovereign liberty to prefer to be the servant rather than the lord of the household, to merrily taunt the gods of power, prestige, honor and recognition, to refuse to take oneself seriously (or anyone who takes himself seriously), to live without gloom by a lackey's agenda, to dance to the tune of a different drummer and be captivated with joy and wonder at the vision and lifestyle of the Ebed Yahweh — these are the revolutionary attitudes that bear the stamp of genuine and unmistakeable discipleship. So central is Jesus' teaching on humble apprenticeship and serving love as the royal road to the Kingdom that at the final judgment, God himself disappears and is visible only in our brothers and sisters: "What you did for those around you, you did for me." I would rather be numbered among the little band who have at least learned this from Jesus and the Bible, than among the legalizers, moralizers and hair-splitters who are so busy straining the gnat that they swallow the camel. Would not this radical, revolutionary and thoroughly orthodox mind-set plunge us into a new Pentecost that would renew the face of the earth? There is simply no sense in trumpeting the Lordship of Jesus if his attitudes, values and behavior are not recognizable in our lives.

According to Paul, the only criterion for greatness in the new Israel of God is the faith that expresses itself in love. The Apostle (who understood the mind of Jesus better than any man or woman who has ever lived) echoes the teaching of Christ in the Upper Room: "You call me Master and Lord, and rightly; so I am. If I, then, the Lord and Master, have washed your feet, you should wash each other's feet. I have given you an example so that you may copy what I have done for you." (Jn. 13:14-15)

"There is no point in getting into an argument about this question of loving. It is what Christianity is all about — take it or leave it. Christianity is not about ritual and moral living except insofar as these two express the love that causes both of them. We must at least pray for the grace to become love."[3]

The spell of self-hatred cast by moralism/ legalism is broken when a Christian is no longer seduced by secular standards of human greatness and makes the glorious breakthrough into the lackey lifestyle of the Master and desires to serve rather than be served. The stark realism of the Gospel allows for no romanticized idealism or sloppy sentimentality here. Servanthood is not an emotion or mood or feeling; it is a decision to live the life of Jesus. It has nothing to do with what we feel; it has everything to do with what we do — humble service. When this metanoia is effected in our lives by the power of the Spirit, freedom from the tyranny of self-hatred is the first fruit. "It was for liberty that Christ freed us. So stand firm and do not take on yourselves the yoke of slavery a second time." (Ga. 5:1)

"There is no church on earth, no evangelist, no accident of time or culture that could create a man or a message like this. To listen carefully to these words is to draw close to the Jesus of the Gospels."[4]

On the afternoon of January 16, 1979, I was reading the Scriptures in my room at the Franciscan Retreat Center in Tampa, Florida. The words of 22-year-old John McEnroe to the umpire at the 1981 Wimbledon Tennis Classic could have been directed to me: "You're the pits, man, the pits!" (He was fined $7000 for abusive language. The double standard of profanity in professional sports raises an intriguing question: if 'pits' is so indelicate to an umpire's ear, why isn't baseball's Billy Martin bankrupt, why don't Tom Lasorda's semaphores lead to a lawsuit, and why isn't football's Don Coryell in jail?) The subtle dominion of self-hatred had returned and I was back on the roller coaster ride of perfectionist depression, neurotic guilt and emotional instability. The despotic power of my idealized self and the nagging litany of "I should have, I could have, I ought to have, why didn't I, why did I" persuaded me that my life and ministry were vitiated by vanity, insensitivity and self-centeredness.

Jesus set me free.

I was reading the pericope of the washing of the feet in John 13. Suddenly I was transported in faith into the Upper Room and took Judas' place among the Twelve. The Servant had tied a towel round his waist, poured water from a pitcher into a copper basin and reached out to wash my feet. (The dress and duty are those of a slave). Involuntarily I pulled my foot back. I could not look at him. I had betrayed the vision, been unfaithful to my dream and thus unfaithful to his plan. He placed his hand on my knee and said:

"Brennan, what these years together have meant to me. You were being held even when you didn't believe I was holding you. I love you, my friend."

Tears rolled down my cheeks. "But Lord, my sins, my repeated failures, my weaknesses . . . "

"I understand. I have been there. Brennan, I expected more failure from you than you expected from yourself." He smiled. "And you always came back. Nothing pleases me so much as when you trust me, when you allow that my compassion is bigger than your sinfulness."

"Jesus, my irritating character defects, the boasting, inflating the truth, the pretenses of being an intellectual, the impatience with people, and all the times I drank to excess . . . "

"What you are saying is true. But your love for me never wavered and your heart remained pure.

What's more, you've done something that over-shadows all the rest. You have been kind to sinners."

I cried — so loud that the priest-retreatant in the adjacent room knocked on the door to ask if I was alright.

"Now, I'll go," Jesus said. "I have just washed your feet. Do the same for others. Serve my people humbly and lovingly. You will find happiness if you do. Peace, my friend."

Jesus, a man like us in all things but ungrate-fulness, our Brother who never knew sin, estranges us from self-hatred through a love that keeps no score of wrongs and a mercy that surpasses human under-standing. In the eyes of the Master we have failed, we detect the infinite compassion of the Father and see revealed the human face of God.

Father John O'Grady writes: "The savior knows that we have failures, even when we have committed ourselves to him. The savior redeems us from all personal failure by telling his followers that in spite of our sin we have value in the eyes of God the Father. A new possibility exists. We can be more than we are at any one moment; we can always bring some sense of goodness to the fore and come closer to living the way that will bring us peace. Even in the midst of personal failure the one who has been saved knows that he or she is still precious in the eyes of God, of Jesus and of his holy community. The one who has been saved knows no sense of isolation. Jesus is the friend who will never fail, the faithful one who will never be lacking in fidelity, even when people are unfaithful to him."[5]

The Gospel portrait of Jesus is that of a strikingly cheerful person who cherished life and existence, and especially other people, as loving gifts from the Father's hand. The peripheral figures whom Jesus encounters in his ministry react in various ways to his presence and message but never with gloom or sadness. In a remarkable passage Edward Schillebeeckx explains the non-fasting of the disciples.[6] Fasting was a sign of mourning and sorrow. It was not that his disciples *did not* fast; they *could not* fast. This was not a matter of canonical dispensation like the Friday abstinence during Lent. It was a question of the existential impossibility of being sad in the living presence of Jesus. The sinners and low-life rejects found that sharing a meal with the Master was a liberating experience of sheer joy. He estranged them from self-hatred with reassuring words such as "Do not live in fear, little flock; don't be afraid, fear is useless, stop worrying, cheer up — your sins are all forgiven." His contagious joy (only carriers can pass it on) in the lavish, gratuitous and indiscriminate love of his heavenly Father infected and liberated his listeners. (If Jesus sat at your dining room table tonight with full knowledge of everything you are and are not; if he laid out your whole life story with the hidden agenda and the dark desires unknown even to yourself, it would still be impossible to be saddened in his presence.) "Experiencing God's love in Jesus Christ means experiencing that one has been unreservedly accepted, approved and infinitely loved, that one can and should accept oneself and one's neighbor. Salvation is joy in God which expresses itself in joy in and with one's neighbor."[7]

To me it is unthinkable to picture a woodenfaced, stoic and joyless Jesus as he blesses the little children. To perceive the human personality of Jesus as a purely passive mask for the dramatic speeches

of divinity is to rob him of his humanity, encase him
in plaster of Paris and conclude that he neither
laughed, cried, smiled or got hurt but simply passed
through our world without emotional engagement.

Mark records that a group of parents, who
obviously sensed something of God's love in Jesus,
wanted him to bless their little ones. The irritated
disciples, fatigued by the long day's journey on foot
from Capernaum to the district of Judea and the far
side of the Jordan, attempted to shoo away the
children. Jesus becomes visibly upset and probably
with a withering glance silences the twelve. The
Evangelist Mark carefully notes that the Lord picked
them up one by one, cradled them, and gave each of
them his blessing.

"I am so glad Jesus didn't suggest they group all
the children together for a sort of general blessing
because he was rather tired. Instead, he took time to
hold each child close to his heart and to earnestly pray
for them all . . . then they joyfully scampered off to
bed. One is tenderly reminded of a beautiful messianic
passage from the prophets: 'He will feed his flock like
a shepherd, he will gather his lambs in his arm, he will
carry them in his bosom, and will gently lead those
that have their young.' (Is. 40:11 TAB) . . . I think
there is a lesson here for anyone who would seek to
set any kind of false condition concerning just who
should be the recipients of God's grace. He blessed
them all!"[8]

It's staggering, mind-blowing, but it's true. Jesus
takes the initiative in seeking out the ungodly, even on
Sunday morning. His loving visitation ends ungodli-
ness and makes the sinner worthy. It is difficult to
understand how anyone has the right to declare
limited access to the Eucharistic table so that certain

people cannot come to Jesus without their consent and approval. Surely there would be abuses but abuses do not take away the reality. "In Jesus the goodness outweighed the evil that surrounded him . . . Sinners are always welcome; tax collectors, prostitutes and anyone else who feels left out can find company with Jesus as the forgiving savior . . . no one was excluded; no one need feel left out."[9]

What would the church be like if we erred from an excess of compassion rather than from a stingy and legalistic lack of it? My intuition is that the Christian community would share something of the mystical vision of Juliana of Norwich who uttered what may be the loveliest and most consoling sentence I have ever read: "And all thing shall be well; and all thing shall be well; and all manner of thing shall be well!"[10]

Jesus perceived that the only way people would experience life as gracious gift, the only way to help them to prize themselves as grace and treasure, was to treat them as treasure and be gracious to them. I can be anointed, prayed over, sermonized to, dialogued with and exposed to God's unconditional love in books, tracts and tapes, but this marvelous revelation will fall on ears that do not hear and eyes that do not see, unless some other human being refresh the weariness of my defeated days. Barring prevenient grace, I simply will not accept my life and being as God's gracious gift, unless someone values me. "We can only sense ourselves and our world valued and cherished by God when we feel valued and cherished by others."[11]

One of the most beautiful chapters in the script that is the story of Jesus of Nazareth is his relationship with Mary Magdalene. (A brief digression: tonight I interrupted writing to attend an AA meeting at Indian Rocks Beach. Driving along the Gulf of Mexico, I picked up a 20-year-old female hitchhiker. After a greeting she immediately told me of her resentment for her live-in boy friend. Both are heavy cocaine users and he demanded that she prostitute herself with his friends to support their habit. I asked her, "Have you turned to God and asked him to help you?" In a breezy nonchalant voice she replied, "Oh I know that God loves me." She did not know. At best she had what Cardinal Newman called "notional" knowledge but not real knowledge. She would experience God in a real way and come to see her life as gracious gift if her boy friend valued her the way Jesus valued Mary Magdalene.)

This is the Christ of my own interiority; the Deliverer from self-hatred through love. At the dinner in the home of Simon the Pharisee Magdalene (presuming she is the sinful woman mentioned) was awed by the loveliness and compassion of this magnetic man. His eyes had called out to her, "Come to me. Come now. Don't wait until you have your act cleaned up and your head on straight. Don't delay until you think you are properly disposed and free of pride and lust, jealousy and self-hatred. Come to me in your brokenness and sinfulness with your fears and insecurities and I will comfort you. I will come to you right where you live and love you just the way you are, just the way you are and not the way you think you should be."

Jesus had convinced her that "winter had passed, that the rains were over and gone," (Sg. 2:1), that her sins had been forgiven and that God now accepted her and approved of her. The moment she surrendered in faith, love took effect and her life was transformed. The result was the inner healing of her heart manifested as peace, joy, gratitude and love. The love of Christ called the sinful woman to enter into the mystery of herself, to abandon clarity, "the kind of clarity the ego seeks, the kind of clarity which comforts me and allows me to think that all I really am is what I *think* I am, and that's all there is to it."[12] The creative power of Jesus' love called Magdalene to regard herself as He did, to see in herself the possibilities which he saw in her. "The place that Mary Magadlene occupies in Christian thought is not due to her strange, deep love for Jesus, but rather to what was wrought in her by Christ's love for her. It was Christ's love for her that delivered her from her past and made her what she became. The central truth for which Mary's life has come to stand is that it is possible to be delivered, through love, from the lowest depths to the shining heights where God dwelleth."[13]

The same theme is re-played with Peter. The compassion of Jesus reaches its zenith in their dialogue on the shores of the Sea of Tiberias. Only the risen Lord sounded the depths of Peter's hurt, guilt and self-hatred. Only Jesus fully understood that there was no treachery in Peter's denial; just a temporary loss of nerve. Like a Marine in combat for the first time, the instinct for self-preservation had prevailed. The purity of Peter's heart and the quality of his love were not debatable or open to question in spite of his betrayal. But Jesus had to rid the Apostle of his clarity, of his limited self-perception, of the debased self-image of who he thought he was. There would be healing from self-hatred for Peter that morning.

Jesus said, "Simon, son of John, do you love me more than these?" "Yes, lord," he said, you know that I love you." At which Jesus said, "Feed my lambs." A second time he put his question, "Simon, son of John, do you love me?" "Yes, Lord," Peter said, you know that I love you." Jesus replied, "Tend my sheep." A third time, Jesus asked him, "Simon, son of John, do you love me?" Peter was hurt because he had asked a third time, "Do you love me?" So he said to him, "Lord, you know everything. You know well that I love you." Jesus said to him, "Feed my sheep."

Jesus not only frees Peter from self-hatred by allowing him to publicly repudiate his triple denial but in the subtlest act of affirmation conceivable, he appoints him leader of his church and entrusts him to preach the Good News with supreme authority in the power of the Spirit.

"I don't know what Peter felt at that moment, but if it's anything like I have experienced with the Lord, it is like this:" Father George Montague S.M., writes, "God I don't even know how to be a fisher of men, now you want me to be a shepherd. I don't even know how to fish, Lord, without you, how am I going to shepherd these people? I don't know how. Jesus didn't say anything more, what he said was enough. Do you love me? Can you allow my love to touch you in your weakness, and set you free there, and empower you there. So that when Peter went out from then on empowered by Jesus, *the only power he had was Jesus love for him* (italics mine) and his love for the Lord. That's the only power that he had, and Jesus wanted to strip him even of his power to fish, and any of his other self-confidences except that God is love and God's power has been given to me in my

weakness. Peter told and retold the story of his own
weakness and how the Lord touched him. When Peter
preached, he preached from his weakness the power
of God. And that is what converted the Roman world
and what will convert us, and the people around us if
they see that the power of God has touched us."[14]

The unflinching, unwavering love and compassion of Jesus Christ, the stranger to self-hatred, is the
ultimate source of our healing and wholeness. This
was the experience of Jesus' followers. This was the
kind of impact he had upon them. This is the real
Jesus inscribed on every page of the gospels. If we
wish to treat him as our God, we must let him be who
he wants to be for us. Returning to Rohr's observa-
tion, we have to conclude that man is made to know
how God longs to love and serve him, to free and
forgive, to heal and make whole his children.

Does the church have any more urgent ministry
than providing time and making space for the critical
question of the Johannine Christ, "Do you love me?"
Is there any credal, codal or cultic priority that
supersedes the personal relationship between the believer and Jesus Christ? Is there any hope for radical
Christian renewal and the implementation of the
social gospel if Jesus Christ is not Lord of my life? Do
we set this decisive question aside in favor of
moralizing, philosophizing, organizing and erecting
new temples to an unknown god?

"The criterion by which Christ assesses his
friends and repudiators is still 'Do you love me?'
What do we make of the Bible if we forget this, even if
we hold to everything else? How can one muster the
melancholy courage, the incredible hard-heartedness,
the insipid stupidity, to inflate demythologizing, his-

torical criticism, and existentialist interpretation
into such a bogey that Jesus' question takes a back
place?"[15]

Though it is repetitive, my own glimpse of Jesus
remains remote if I do not allude to that winter's
night, December 13, 1968, in the cave in the Zaragoza
desert in Spain. The world was asleep but my heart
was awake to the Lord. In faith, I heard Jesus say,
"For love of you I left my Father's side. I came to you
who ran from me, who fled me, who did not want to
hear my name. For love of you I was covered with
spit, punched and beaten and fixed to the wood of
the cross."

Those words are burned on my life. Whether in
the state of grace or dis-grace, the words impose
themselves with the stark realism of objective truth.
I stared at the crucifix for hours, figuratively saw the
blood streaming from every wound and pore in
Christ's body, and I heard the cry of his blood: "This
is not a joke. It is not a laughing matter to me
that I have loved you." The longer I looked the more
I realized that no man has ever loved me and no
woman could ever love me as he does. I cried out in
the darkness, "Jesus, are you crazy, are you out of
your mind to have loved me so much?" I learned that
night what a wise old Franciscan told me the day I
joined the Order: "Once you come to know the love of
Jesus Christ, nothing else in the world will seem
beautiful or desirable."

Ironically, it was the same day, December 13th,
twelve years later that I went to pray in the parish
Church in Tamarac, Florida at two in the afternoon.
The usual tenor of my prayer-life is dryness, longing
and experiencing the absence of God in the hope of

communion. The moment I knelt down, my mind was filled with the image of a three-year-old boy playing on the rug in his living room. Off in the corner his mother was sitting on the floor in the lotus position knitting. She dropped her working and beckoned to him. He toddled over and climbed up on her knees. She looked down and asked softly, "How much do you love me?" he extended his tiny arms as far as they would go and exclaimed, "This much I love you." In an instant it was thirty years later; the little boy in the fulness of manhood hung nailed to a crossbeam. His mother looked up and said, "How much do you love me? His arms were stretched out to the ends of the universe. "This much I love you." And he died.

We turn once again to the pivotal question: Who Is Jesus? Everything else is a distraction. He is the crucified one. "He is unmistakeable and identifiable with Jesus of Nazareth only as the man of the cross."[16] It is the signature of the risen one, and it follows that a Christian is only a disciple as long as he stands in the shadow of the cross.

It is inevitable that when you hang with bad company, you get a bad reputation. Is there anything more precious to us than our good name? Our standing in the community is not a minor matter. What would people think if you were frequently seen in the company of prostitutes, drug dealers and slumlords? Jesus mixed easily with the nobodies, the discards and the lowlife rejects. He mingled with tax collectors who were downright sinners — "miserable sinners in the proper sense of the term, practicing a proscribed trade, odious cheats and swindlers, grown rich in the service of the occupying power, afflicted with permanent uncleanness as collaborators and traitors to the national cause, incapable of repentance because they simply could not remember how many they had cheated or how much was involved. And such professional swindlers were the very people with whom Jesus had to get involved."[17]

In the culture of first century Palestine, being seen in the presence of women not of one's family implied only one thing. Jesus' friendliness with a number of women, especially prostitutes, muddied whatever good name he still had left. "He was not afraid of creating a scandal or losing his reputation or even losing his life. All the men of religion, even John the Baptist, were scandalized by the way he mixed socially with sinners, by the way he seemed to enjoy their company, by his permissiveness with regard to the laws, by his apparent disregard for the seriousness of sin and by his free and easy way of treating God . . . Jesus did nothing and compromised on nothing for the sake of even a modicum of prestige in the eyes of others. He did not seek anyone's approval, not even the approval of the greatest man born of woman."[18]

I find myself threatened, challenged and exhilarated by Christ's freedom from human respect, his extraordinary independence, indomitable courage and unparalleled authenticity. In preaching the gospel I have been graced to speak fearlessly in the knowledge and conviction that the Word of God must not be fettered, compromised or watered down; but in my personal life, my fears and insecurities lead me voraciously to seek the approval of others, to assume a defensive posture when I am unjustly accused, to feel guilty over refusing any request, to doggedly live up to others' expectations, to be all things to all men in a way that would make St. Paul shudder.

"Powerful others will try to make me conform and live up to their expectations. I may have to run the risk of being defiant, of standing up to, and of going against powerful others. I am called to stand on my own two feet and to develop the ability to say yes or no in making decisions for the emergence of my life. To be seduced from following my path is to be controlled by others, to become a people pleaser, and to be ruled by the tyrannical demands of others. Failure to stand up to others and to assume responsibility for the direction of my life and the promotion of love in light of God's design for me should engender healthy guilt."[19]

I cannot free myself. I must be set free. Yes, the untrammelled freedom of Jesus disturbs me, his utter indifference to human respect makes me uncomfortable; but he invites me to make friends with my insecurities, smile at them, outgrow them in patient endurance, live with the serene confidence that he never abandons his friends even when we disappoint him, and look forward in expectant faith to the day when I can say to the angry chairperson of the Inscrutable Noonies Society whose speaking invitation I have just refused: "Frankly, my dear, I don't give a damn."

It can be unequivocally stated that the central, most important theme in the personal life of Jesus, the theme that lies at the very heart of the revelation that he is, is his growing trust, intimacy and love of his Abba, his heavenly Father. The interior life of Christ was completely Father-centered. The master clue for interpreting the gospel narrative, the foundation of Jesus' compelling demands, the source of his towering zeal was his personal experience of God as Abba. "The overtones of this small word will always remain beyond us. Yet we sense in it something of the closeness of Jesus with his Father. We touch in it the very heart of his personality. The Abba experience made him the person he was. It freed him from all self-concern and enabled him to relate to each and every person with great ease, openness, sympathy and a liberating love."[20]

The pearl of great price in my life, the most treasured gift I have ever received from Jesus is to come to know the Father. "No one knows the Son except the Father, just as no one knows the Father except the Son and those to whom the Son chooses to reveal him" (Mt. 11:27). Joachim Jeremias does not hesitate to say that this is the central revelation of the New Testament.

Jesus brought a revolution in the understanding of God. It is impossible to exaggerate the extravagance of the Father's compassion and love. The god of Ruller — Something Awful — and all other false images are blown away. Projection is exposed for the idolatry that it is. To pray to any god other than a Father who finds sheer delight in reconciliation is illusion, cowardice and superstition. For the disciple, God is no other than as he is seen in the person of Jesus. "He who sees me sees the Father" (Jn. 14:9).

The love of the Father for his children plunges us into mystery because it is utterly beyond the pale of human experience. The parable of the Prodigal reveals a love that is gratuitous. Let us suppose that you financed your youngest son through an Ivy League University; room, board, tuition, spending money and plane tickets home to the tune of $60,000 over four years. He graduates. You host a lavish party for two hundred of his friends and classmates — champagne, caviar, pizza and Ripple wine, baked Alaska and Twinkies. The Beach Boys and Alice Cooper are flown in to provide the music. The celebration breaks up at dawn. You sit before the fireplace with your son and inquire if he enjoyed the night.

"I'm going to level with you," he answers. "I can't stand you, your values or your face. Tomorrow my insurance policy matures and I'm splitting. I've got my diploma and that's my passport to fat city. Goodbye."

You are stunned and brokenhearted, but you know you can't stop him. He leaves. For the next three years, you literally do not know if he is dead or alive. No calls or postcards; the police can't find a trace of him. One Monday morning at three a.m., your doorbell rings. You trip downstairs and open the door in shock. Your son is standing on the steps, booze on his breath, lipstick on his collar, his clothes dishevelled. What would you do? Would you fall on your son's neck, smother him with tears and kisses, throw on the lights, call to your spouse and shout, "Break out the Dom Perignon we've been saving and play Handel's Messiah. Bobby's home. He's not dead; he's alive."

Your neighbors would deem you foolish and stupid. But Jesus says: that is the way my Father is. He wants you home more than you want to be home. His love knows no bounds. Never compare your pallid, capricious, conditional human love with my Father's love. He is God not man.

"Try, if you please, to invent a different ending for this story. Make the old man rebuff the boy at first; have him stand on his dignity and require of the rascal proofs of his change of heart; let him read a sermon on wild oats before the forgiving kiss is bestowed; have him take the penitent at his word — as he richly deserves to be taken — and try him out with the slaves for a year or two, till the family pride, or outraged justice, is satisfied. Imagine, in short, *any possible ending but this,* and you have destroyed the noblest picture of redeeming grace ever created, and lowered God to the level of man's virtue. Heathen religions in plenty, and some versions of the Christian religion, furnish us with the alternatives suggested above; Christ alone shows us the suffering Father who saves by forgiving."[21]

Jesus is the human face of the Father.

Though it is remarkably easy to call God 'Abba', it is almost impossible to live. To pray, 'thy will be done' from the bowels of your being requires a great deal. It cost Jesus his life. To do the perceived will of God in all circumstances and relationships enjoins radical obedience to the Word who said, "I come to do your will, O God." It was Jesus' food and he demands the same diet of his followers.

The phrase, thy will be done, occurs in only four places in the New Testament — all in the context of martyrdom. The three passion narratives in the Synoptics[22] refer explicitly to Jesus' impending death. Paul announces he is ready for martyrdom in Acts 21:13-14: "Why are you crying and breaking my heart in this way? For the name of the Lord Jesus I am prepared not only for imprisonment, but for death, in Jerusalem. Since he would not be dissuaded we said nothing further except, *"The Lord's will be done."* For Paul, death was not terminal but the final breakthrough into the open, waiting, outstretched arms of the Abba of Jesus. In the non-canonical writing, *the Martyrdom of Polycarp,*[22] the soldiers seize him and begin to beat him about the face and body. Polycarp cries out, "May God's will be done," and the martyrdom begins.

The Father's will is a river of life flowing into Jesus, inundating his being. It is a bloodstream from which he draws life even more profoundly than he draws life from his mother. And whoever stands at the ready in obedient love becomes a part of this bloodstream. He is united to Jesus more deeply than the way in which Jesus was united to his mother.

To acknowledge that our Father is the source of all life and holiness makes gratitude the most characteristic attitude of the child of God. The petition, "Give us this day our daily bread" means the awareness of our dependence and the acceptance of all of life as God's gracious gift. It strikes down possessiveness and makes us conscious that we are beggars. How reluctant we are to receive the gift! We stake out our own piece of turf, claim it as our own, become grasping, anxious and care-ridden about the security of our baubles, trinkets, golf balls and immaculate lawns. "We gather into barns, insure the barns and their contents, buy a German Shepherd or hire a security guard, and try to see to it that Blacks do not build barns in the same area."[23] We sell ourselves to the gods of security, sensation and power, and a sickness enters the very heart of our existence. We grow competitive rather than compassionate, make others our rivals, steppingstones to our enthronement in a palace overlooking Malibu, part of life's expense account, enslaved in the Babylonian captivity of the modern world.

One does not find an attitude of gratitude in the slavemarket.

Jesus brings freedom from the money game, the power game, the pleasure game and the pervasive sense of self-hatred that racks our torn conscience. With insight that defies imagination, he proposes a new agenda that proffers peace and a joy that the world would never dare promise: "Turn to my Father, set your heart on his kingdom, and these other things will be given you as well" (Lk. 12:31).

This is a glimpse of the Jesus that I have met over the years on the slopes of my self, the Christ of my interiority. There is a beauty and enchantment about the Nazarene that draws me irresistibly to follow him. He is the Pied Piper of my lonely heart. It is not pious prattle to say: the only valid reason I can think of for living is Jesus Christ. Paul puts it so well: "There is only Christ and he is everything."

In order to be free to be faithful to this sacred man and his dream, to others and ourselves, we must be liberated from the damnable imprisonment of self-hatred, freed from the shackles of projectionism, perfectionism, moralism/legalism and unhealthy guilt. Freedom for fidelity demands freedom from enslavement.

It is a tired cliche, a battered bumper-sticker, an overused and often superficial slogan, but it is the truth of the Gospel: Jesus is the answer. Is there any price too exorbitant, any cost too extravagant to pay for the privilege of being able to make your own personal response to his haunting question: Who do you say that I am? "I believe that nothing can happen that will outweigh the supreme advantage of knowing Christ Jesus my Lord . . . and I look on everything else as rubbish if only I can have Christ" (Ph. 2:8).

Footnotes

1 Schillebeeckx, *Ibid.* pp. 171-172.

2 Kasemann, *Ibid.* p. 155.

3 Doherty, *Ibid.* p. 211.

4 *Jesus — A Gospel Portrait*, Donald Senior, C.P. Pflaum Standard, Cincinnati, O. 1975. p. 57.

5 *Models of Jesus*, John F. O'Grady, Doubleday & Co. Inc., Garden City, N.Y. 1981. pp. 146-147.

6 Schillebeeckx, *Ibid.* pp. 204-205.

7 Kasper, *Ibid.* p. 86.

8 *Our Heavenly Father*, Robert Frost. Logos International Plainfield, N.J. 1978. p. 44.

9 O'Grady, *Ibid.* p. 161.

10 *Sadhana, a Way to God*, Anthony de Mello, S.J., Institute of Jesuit Sources, St. Louis, Mo. 1978. p. 134.

11 *Jesus, the Man and the Myth*, James P. Mackey. Paulist Press, N.Y., N.Y. 1979. p. 170.

12 *The Forgiveness of Sin*, Tad Guzie & John McIlhon. Thomas More Press, Chicago, Il. 1979. p. 38.

13 *Christ and the Fine Arts*, Cynthia Pearl Maus. Harper and Row, N.Y., N.Y. 1938. p. 215.

14 *Healing*, George Montague, C.M. This quote is taken from his teaching at the charismatic conference, Notre Dame, Ind. May, 1981.

15 Kasemann, *Ibid.* p. 147.

16 *Perspectives on Paul*, E. Kasemann. Fortress Press, Philadelphia, Pa. 1971. p. 56.

17 *On Being A Christian*, Hans Kung. Doubleday, N.Y., N.Y. 1976. p. 271.

18 *Jesus Before Christianity*, Albert Nolan, O.P. Orbis Books, Maryknoll, N.Y. 10545. pp. 117-118.

19 *Guilt, Ibid.* p. 109. Vincent M. Billotta III.

20 *Certain as the Dawn*, Peter van Breemen S.J. The author is quoting from his previous work, *Called By Name*. Dimension Books, Denville, N.J. 07834. 1980. p. 31.

21 *Maux, Ibid.* p. 173. Quoted from *The Gospel in Art*, Dr. Bailey, Pilgrim Press, Boston, Mass. p. 173.

22 *The Prayer of Jesus*, notes from a series of lectures by Father Francis Martin at Loyola U., New Orleans, La. July, 1978.

23 Mackey, *Ibid.* pp. 135-136.

THREE

HEALING THROUGH MEAL-SHARING

In the year 1925, if a wealthy plantation owner in Atlanta, Georgia, extended a formal invitation to four colored cotton-pickers to come to his mansion for Sunday dinner, preceded by cocktails and followed by several hours of brandy and conversation, the Georgia aristocracy would have been outraged, neighboring Alabama infuriated, and the KKK apoplectic. The caste system was inviolable, social and racial discrimination inflexible, and indiscretion made the loss of reputation inevitable.

The scandal that Jesus caused in first-century Palestinian Judaism can scarcely be appreciated by the Christian world today. The class system was enforced *de rigueur*. It was legally forbidden to mingle with sinners who were outside the law; the prohibition on table-fellowship with beggars, tax-collectors and prostitutes was a religious, social and cultural taboo. Unfortunately, the meaning of meal-sharing is largely lost on society today. In the east to share a meal with someone is a guarantee of peace, trust, brotherhood and forgiveness; the shared table is a shared life. To say, "I would like to have dinner with you" means to an orthodox Jew, "I would like to enter into friendship with you. Even today an American Jew will share a donut and a cup of coffee with you, but to extend a dinner invitation is to say: "Come to my mikdash me-at, my miniature sanctuary, my dining room table and we will celebrate the most beautiful experience that life affords — friendship." That is what Zacchaues heard when Jesus called him down from the sycamore tree, and that is why Jesus' practice of table-fellowship caused hostile comment from the outset of his ministry.

It did not escape the Pharisees' attention that Jesus meant to befriend the rabble. He was not only breaking the law; he was destroying the very structure of Jewish society! "They all complained when they saw what was happening. He has gone to stay at a sinner's house, they said" (Lk. 19:7). But Zacchaeus, not too hung up on respectability, was overwhelmed with joy.

"It would be impossible to overestimate the impact these meals must have had upon the poor and the sinners. By accepting them as friends and equals Jesus had taken away their shame, humiliation and guilt. By showing them that they mattered to him as people he gave them a sense of dignity and released them from their old captivity. The physical contact which he must have had with them at table (Jn. 13:25) and which he obviously never dreamed of disallowing (Lk. 7:38-39) must have made them feel clean and acceptable. Moreover because Jesus was looked upon as a man of God and a prophet, they would have interpreted his gesture of friendship as God's approval on them. They were now acceptable to God. Their sinfulness, ignorance and uncleanness had been overlooked and were no longer being held against them."[1]

Through table fellowship Jesus ritually acted out his insight into the Father's indiscriminate love — a love that causes his sun to rise on bad men as well as good, and his rain to fall on honest and dishonest men alike (Mt. 5:45). The inclusion of sinners in the community of salvation, achieved in table fellowship, is the most dramatic expression of the message of the redeeming love of the merciful God.

"Several years ago Karl Rahner was giving a lecture in Rome on salvation and remarked that salvation 'is a bottle of coke'. All over Europe there are signs: things go better with coke. Rahner described the experience: The day is hot and the streets of Rome are dusty and filled with exhaust from the buses; you walk along with your friend, you see the sign, sit down and enjoy the comfort and ease of a bottle of coke with your friend. Salvation is a bottle of coke.

"Whatever contributes to the well-being of mankind, whatever is good and noble and lovely and true is the experience of salvation. Salvation is not reserved for the future alone. It is present when a family sits down at a family celebration in thanksgiving for the goodness they have received and the goodness they contribute to each other and enjoy fine food and good wine and great company."[2]

The ordinary meal sharing of Jesus at home and on the road was eucharist, and so should be the thousand meals that a family shares each year. The word eucharist means to give thanks and these meals were grateful celebrations of God's gift of life, celebrated in shared food and joyful fellowship. It seems to have been Jesus' favorite form of recreation. Dinner parties were such a prominent aspect of his routine that, more than once, he was accused of being a drunkard and a glutton.

The thorough research of Albert Nolan O.P. indicates that Jesus had his own home in Capernaum or at least shared one with Peter, Andrew and their families. Undoubtedly, in his ministry of itinerant evangelism, Jesus often slept on the side of the road or stayed with friends. "The Son of man has nowhere to lay his head" (Mk. 8:20). But upon returning from his missionary journeys, he had some kind of quasi-permanent domicile.[3] The phrase, "he *entertained* sinners (Lk. 15:2) suggests that Jesus was often the host and may have rented a hall more than once (as he did at the Last Supper) if the guests were numerous. The guest list would include a rag-tag parade of donkey peddlers, prostitutes, herdsmen, slumlords and gamblers. A social climber Jesus was not!

Status-seekers in today's society are selective about their dinner guests and will make elaborate preparations for people they want to stand well with. They wait anxiously to see if they will be invited in return. Consciously or unconsciously, the power-brokers and social gadflys of our day do not under-estimate the ritual power of meal-sharing. Jesus' sinner-guests were well aware that table fellowship entailed more than mere politeness and courtesy; it meant peace, acceptance, reconciliation, fraternity. "For Jesus this fellowship at table with those whom the devout had written off was not merely the expression of liberal tolerance and humanitarian sentiment. It was the expression of his mission and message: peace and reconciliation for all, without exception, even for the moral failures."[4]

I once met a pastor in the hills of Colorado who invites a family to his rectory every Sunday afternoon for a home-cooked meal. Frequently the guests are unchurched or exchurched. During my visit the fare

was simple but the company and conversation stimu-
lating. This family shared the deep hurt inflicted on
them by a previous pastor and consequently had
discontinued churchgoing. But that afternoon they
received consideration instead of expected condemna-
tion, a merciful acquittal rather than an anticipated
verdict of guilty. They returned to the worshipping
community the following week. They had been healed
by an ordinary Sunday meal. Table-sharing with the
pastor brought them into fellowship with God.

How do we justify the exclusion of divorced
Catholics in invalid marriages from the Lord's Supper
when He hosted sinners and set the table for moral
failures? How long is this really to go on? Admittedly,
the conditions and requirements for obtaining a
canonical annulment have been widened and
broadened, and various attempts continue to be made
by the formulators and administrators of Church law
to mitigate the suffering inflicted by such sanctions,
within limits imposed by the sacramental doctrine.
Yet, "although this procedure has been a source of
some relief, it is clearly a legal makeshift, open to
serious abuses, and basic problems in this area remain
difficult and urgent."[5]

A 68-year-old man in Florida came to me recently for counselling; in fact, he fell into my arms in
tears. He has been deprived of table fellowship with
Jesus in the Eucharist for forty-six years! Wounded at
Anzio Beach in World War II, he was honorably
discharged, returned to the States and in desperate
loneliness married a girl he barely knew in a Catholic
ceremony. Within three weeks she had committed
adultery with several other men and the marriage
ended in divorce. He remarried outside the church
and, as so often happens, the second successful

marriage healed a failed human situation. This elderly man told me he simply did not have the emotional resources to re-open "that can of worms" and endure the painful trauma of a judicial inquiry that might lead to annulment. This old man's name is legion.

The prohibition preventing his return to the sacraments makes it impossible to show compassion. "One finds it difficult to believe that the refusal of compassion reflects the image of Jesus. It seems to put things before people."[6] The guest-list shrinks and the number of empty chairs at the Lord's table grows. Jesus told us to go out to the highways and byways and drag in the beggars, the cripples and the broken-hearted; instead we tell those already seated at the supper table to get up and leave and we shut the door after them.

The Church of Jesus Christ is a home not only for the morally upright but for the moral failures and for those who for a variety of reasons have not been able to honor ecclesiastical teaching. Forty-six years! Even the incestuous man in Corinth was permitted by Paul to return to the community for fear of breaking his spirit and leading him into despair. The Church is a healing community proclaiming the Father's indiscriminate love and unconditional grace, offering pardon, reconciliation and salvation to the downtrodden and leaving the judgment to God.

"A Church that will not accept the fact that it consists of sinful men and exists for sinful men becomes hardhearted, self-righteous, inhuman. It deserves neither God's mercy nor men's trust. But if a Church with a history of fidelity and infidelity, of knowledge and error, takes seriously the fact that it is only in God's Kingdom that the wheat is separated from the tares, good fish from bad, sheep from goats, a holiness will be acknowledged in it by grace which it cannot create for itself. Such a Church is then aware that it has no need to present a spectacle of higher morality to society, as if everything in it were ordered to the best. It is aware that its faith is weak, its knowledge dim, its profession of faith halting, that there is not a single sin or failing which it has not in one way or another been guilty of. And though it is true that the Church must always dissociate itself from sin, *it can never have any excuse for keeping any sinners at a distance.* (Italics mine) If the Church self-righteously remains aloof from failures, irreligious and immoral people, it cannot enter justified into God's kingdom. But if it is constantly aware of its guilt and sin, it can live in joyous awareness of forgiveness. The promise has been given to it that anyone who humbles himself will be exalted."[7]

What to do? Pope John Paul II has announced that the theme of the 1983 Synod of Bishops will be "Penance and Reconciliation in the Mission of the Church." Chosen from several themes that concern the life of the church, penance and reconciliation will consider the subject matter of the encyclicals Redemptor Hominis (Redeemer of Man) and Dives in Misericordia (Rich in Mercy). Archbishop Tomko, secretary of the synod, commented that "reconciliation and penance are seen to be surprisingly relevant today if they are set against some phenomena which, directly or indirectly, are upsetting the cultural situation in the modern world." 1983, it is said, might well be an opportunity for a re-examination of the implementation of the 1973 rite of reconciliation in the dioceses of the United States.

Is that all?

Let the church declare a Jubilee Year in the spirit of the Book of Leviticus and host a homecoming celebration for all disenfranchised ex-Catholics! In Israel every seventh or sabbatical year all debts had to be cancelled; every fiftieth or Jubilee year everything one lost was restored to its original owner and everyone was called to return to his own home. "In this year of jubilee each of you is to return to his ancestral home" (Lv. 25:13). In the sabbatical year "you must permit the land to be redeemed . . . but if he does not acquire sufficient means to buy back his land, what he has sold shall remain in the possession of the purchaser until the jubilee, when it must be released and returned to its original owner" (Lv. 25:24, 28).

In a year of jubilation that echoes with the joy of the gospel, let the leaders of our church proclaim amnesty — unconditional gratuitous pardon for those outside the law; let Jesus' ministry of estranging people from shame, humiliation, rejection and self-hatred be continued; in a magnificent gesture of mercy let the face of a compassionate God be revealed.

As we have seen, Jesus vindicates his table companionship with sinners and justifies his revolutionary conduct to his critics by claiming, 'God's love to the returning sinner knows no bounds. What I do represents God's nature and will.' "Jesus thus claims that in his actions the love of God to the repentant sinner is made effectual."[8] Jesus, by taking sinners into fellowship with him, takes them into fellowship with God. The awareness that God is love continues to be the ultimate reality for Jesus and the basis for his unprecedented socializing with ragamuffins. This has important implications for the liturgical life of the Christian community.

The transcendence of God is the underlying presupposition of Jesus' preaching and the natural overflowing of his own interior life. The classic definition of preaching remains: *aliis contemplata tradere* — to hand on to others the fruits of one's own contemplation. Pere Sertillanges hints at this when he writes: "Let us try to analyze as well as we can the prayer of the Master. To what do his sentiments correspond? What outbursts of soul do they excite? Undoubtedly the first is adoration . . . to adore is to recognize the whole of the object and the nothingness of the adorer . . . Adoration is nonentity swooning away and gladly expiring in the presence of Infinity. And that is what Jesus does. He acknowledges that the creature is nothing, nothing but a breath from the divine mouth. He recognizes that He Himself is nothing from the standpoint of that humanity which He animates, marvelous as it is. 'Why do you call me good?' He said one day to a young man who had addressed Him as good master. 'Only one is good: God.' One alone is also great; and the human Christ, with all his glory, is but a ray broken loose from God. By adoration then, He reascended humbly toward His source."[9]

This consciousness of the Father's awesome holiness, total otherness and mysterious greatness fires his diatribes against the Pharisees who had presumed to box God in in the Torah and figure him out in the Talmud. However, this is not Jesus' dominant awareness of God. God was not viewed primarily in terms of power, knowledge, beauty or otherness. He is Abba, he is love. Calling God 'Abba' reveals what is new in Jesus understanding of God: God is close to men in love. Hence, the privileged path for gaining access to God is love.

The parish Eucharistic liturgy is a public communal expression of the love of God and neighbor: any cultic action that stands in the way of love stands in the way of God himself. The Eucharistic celebration is meant to achieve what Jesus effected in table fellowship — thanksgiving, peace, mutual acceptance, reconciliation, fraternity. When eucharistic communities continue to harbor grudges one toward another, and nurture resentments, when cool cordiality and polite indifference flourish, when cliques and splinter groups abound and the lines of social, religious and ethnic divisions are reinforced, these liturgies shore up rather than tear down the barriers that divide people and diminish the quality of life. The Eucharist is celebrated unworthily. "Worship, cult and religion in general have no absolute autonomy of their own for Jesus. His God is not an egocentric being. He is a being for others, not a being for himself alone. Cultic worship is not only hypocritical but absolutely meaningless if it is not accompanied by love for other people; for in such a case it cannot possibly be a way of corresponding to God."[10]

At a cocktail party in the midwest two years ago, six couples were standing in a circle sipping martinis. A husband turned to his wife and said, "You're getting so fat I am embarrassed to take you out any more." What she heard was, "You don't love me any more." The husband is a Eucharistic minister in his parish and emulated as a model Catholic. By whose standards? According to Jesus' reply to the lawyer in Matthew 22, the only norm for a good and faithful disciple is that he be a professional lover of God and people. Nothing at all can be set over in opposition to right relationships between human beings.

"So then, if you are bringing your offering to the altar and there remember that your brother has something against you, leave your offering there before the altar, go and be reconciled with your brother first, and then come back and present your offering" (Mt. 5:23-24). What a terrifying reversal of religious priorities! The worship of God and the time of cult are subordinated to reconciliation with one's brother; the value of the liturgical action in the sight of God, independent of the caliber of the music, the effectiveness of the homily and the imaginative design of the banners, is measured by the quality of life and love in the eucharistic community. This could be as scandalous to the devout Christian as was Jesus' table fellowship with sinners to the devout Jew.

What enormous potential for healing lies within the worshipping community! If what was said earlier is true — that we can only experience the compassion and unconditional acceptance of Jesus Christ when we feel valued and cherished by others — then it is the parish family itself that effects the healing of self-hatred for the divorcees, drunks, scalywags and social misfits burdened with emotional and mental disorders. The quality of a Christian's presence in the eucharistic assembly not only to God but to his brothers and sisters is what Paul meant by 'recognizing the Body.' His warmth and congeniality, nonjudgmental attitude and welcoming love may well be the catalyst allowing the healing power of Jesus to become operative in the life of an alienated forlorn brother. This winsome wedding of liturgy and life reactualizes Jesus table fellowship with sinners and brings healing and wholeness to the entire community.

Footnotes

[1] Nolan, *Ibid.* p. 39.

[2] *Jesus, Lord and Christ, Ibid.* p. 81.

[3] Nolan. Ibid. p. 38.

[4] Kung. *Ibid.* p. 273.

[5] Gaffney. *Ibid.* p. 256.

[6] *The New Testament Without Illusion,* John McKenzie. Thomas More Press, Chicago, Il. 1980. p. 155.

[7] King. *Ibid.* p. 507-508.

[8] *The Parables of Jesus,* Joachim Jeremias. Charles Scribner's sons, N.Y., N.Y. 1970. p. 132.

[9] *Jesus,* A. D. Sertillanges, English edition, Dimension Books, Denville, N.J. 07834. 1976. p. 36.

[10] *Christology at the Crossroads, A Latin American Approach,* Jon Sobrino S.J. Orbis Books, Maryknoll, N.Y. 1978. p. 167.

FOUR

DELIVERANCE THROUGH STORY-TELLING

The eleventh step of the AA program reads: "Sought to improve my conscious contact with God through prayer and meditation, seeking only the knowledge of his will for us and the power to carry it out." After delivering, what I considered to be, a dazzling explanation of the step — an interpretation filled with profound theological, spiritual and metaphysical insights, a woman at the meeting approached me and said, "I loved your story about the strawberry." "Yuk," says I. "Ugh," says she. Silently, we nodded in clandestine agreement that one humble strawberry had more power than all my pompous inanities.

There is an extraordinary power in story-telling that stirs the imagination and makes an indelible impression on the mind. Malcolm Muggeridge overstates his case to make this point: "only mystics, clowns and artists, in my experience, speak the truth, which, as Blake keeps insisting is perceptible to the imagination rather than the mind. Our knowledge of Jesus Christ is far too serious a business to be left to theologians and exegetes alone. From the Middle

Ages these professionals have monotonously neglected art and the imagination as guides to religious truth. I find myself in complete agreement with those who wish to reinstate the mystics, clowns and artists alongside the scholars. The imaginable is the believable. To modify Wittgenstein: What we cannot imagine, we must confine to silence and non-belief."[1]

To move through the language and imagery of Jesus' parables offers some fascinating insights into his sensibilities. Noah Webster defines an iconoclast as "one who makes attacks on cherished beliefs and institutions, one who destroys or opposes the veneration of religious images." Jesus, the master storyteller, was an iconoclast. His parables expressed in words what occurred in his actions. He shattered idols and blew away preconceived ideas of who God is and what man is meant to be.

The parables of divine mercy — the lost coin, the lost sheep and the lost son — are rooted in Jesus' own experience of his Father. He speaks wholly and entirely in virtue of this reality. The stories were intended not only to defend his notorious conduct with sinners, but to startle his critics and stand them on their heads by cracking through their conventional way of thinking about God. Jesus challenged the one-dimensionality of the Pharisees who gleefully anticipated a Day of Wrath from which they would be spared because of their orthodoxy and unfaltering piety. Deeply offending by the gospel of reprieve for the wretched, they excoriated Jesus as an irreligious man who did not walk in God's way.

Jesus skewered his opponents with words to the effect: The harlots who have no imagined righteousness to protect will be dancing into the kingdom while you have your alleged virtue burnt out of you! Hear me well: I have come to announce the dawn of a new age, an era of incredible generosity. Allow yourselves to be captivated by joy and wonder at the surpassing greatness of my Father's love for the lost; set it over against your own joyless, loveless, thankless and self-righteous lives. Let go of your impoverished understanding of God and your circumscribed notion of morality. Strike out in a new direction. Cease from your loveless way and be compassionate. Celebrate the homecoming of the lost and rejoice in my Father's munificence."

Here there is more than deliverance from self-hatred for the Christian who interiorizes and appropriates to himself the meaning of these three stories of the Master. There is holiness. "To be a disciple, and thus different from the unconverted pagan, means being as the heavenly Father is: perfect," writes the Scripture scholar Donald Senior C.P.; "Luke uses the word 'merciful.' (6:36) Both terms can be reduced to the same reality. For 'perfect' in Matthew's context means 'whole, complete.' To be whole or complete, as the Father is complete, means loving with limitless compassion . . . Following Jesus in his ministry of compassion defines the meaning of 'being perfect as your heavenly Father is perfect.'"[2]

These parables of the Storyteller do not shine; they burn. They force us to rethink our faith, get in touch with the God of our own interiority and re-examine our attitudes toward self and others. The earthy imagery and language have such a hypnotic appeal to the imagination that they prevent us from not thinking about them. Slowly a sense of foreboding surfaces. Is this Good News too good to be true? Do I want to throw in with the Nazarene? Who is this Storyteller anyway? Is Yahweh actually revealing himself to me in this teller of parables? Is God's mercy in fact manifested in a definitive and decisive way through Jesus of Nazareth? Besides, what kind of lunatic justice is this that gives preferential treatment to a shiftless bum over his hardworking, nose-to-the-grindstone brother? And that other story he told about the guys who worked only an hour and got the same pay as those who had put in an eight-hour day. Is that fair play? I'm not against lending a helping hand but that wacko Samaritan really overdid it. Helping a man who has been mugged out of the gutter is one thing, but putting him up in a motel and picking up the tab for his room and meals? There goes my beer money for the month! The real crunch is the butler who went to the slammer because he wouldn't let the maid off the hook for three lousy bucks . . .

The Storyteller unsettles us. His parables bluntly question our traditional image of God, challenge our invulnerable stands of rectitude and justice, and open up the possibility of a radically new lifestyle that stands in stark contrast to our conventional behavior. Jesus confronts us with a choice: embrace the message disclosed in the parables or reject it and march to the music of your own drummer. Open up to letting yourself be loved by my Father and living a life of compassion or return to the regime of secure piety and well-regulated virtue.

Unrelentingly, Jesus stands by his stories and calls out to us for trusting faith, as he did to his Jewish listeners two thousand years ago. Again and again they persisted: Why do you do this? What makes a prophet associate with riff-raff, shunned by all respectable people?

"And he replies: Because they are sick and need me, because they are truly repentant, and because they feel the gratitude of children forgiven by God. Because, on the other hand, you, with your loveless, self-righteous, disobedient hearts, have rejected the gospel. But, above all, because I know what God is like, so good to the poor, so glad when the lost are found, so overflowing with a father's love for the returning child, so merciful to the despairing, the helpless and the needy. That is why!"[3]

Paradoxically, it is another set of stories, known as the 'crisis' parables that Jesus employs to set his people free from the bondage of self-hatred. The urgency to act is the message of these parables. They issue a cry of warning, a summons to repentance because of the lateness of the hour. Jesus says, You are having a hurricane party and the tidal wave is approaching. "You are feasting and dancing — on the volcano which may erupt at any moment."[4] The impending crisis precludes procrastination. In a variety of similes, The Master says, "Stay awake, because you do not know when the master of the house is coming, evening, midnight, cockcrow, dawn; if he comes unexpectedly, he must not find you asleep. And what I say to you I say to all: 'Stay awake!'" (M4. 14:33-37).

The implication of Luke 12:35-40 is unmistakable. "See to it that you are dressed for action and have your lamps lit. Be like men awaiting their master to return from a wedding feast. Happy those servants whom the master finds awake when he comes . . . You too must stand ready, because the Son of Man is coming at an hour you do not expect."

In the parable of the wedding feast, the guest without a wedding garment is forcibly seized by the bouncers and heaved out the door. "The festal garment is repentance. Put it on today before your death, the day before the Deluge breaks, put it on today! The demand of the crisis is conversion."[5]

Rome is burning, Jesus says. Drop your fiddle, change your life and come to me. Let go of nostalgia and mourning for the good old days that never were anyway. A Latin liturgy in which you never participated, traditional virtues you never practiced, legalistic obedience you never honored and a sterile orthodoxy you never accepted. The old era is done. The decisive inbreak of God has happened.

The Christian who realizes the gravity of his situation knows that the decision brooks no delay. The Storyteller calls us not to fear but to action. Procrastination only prolongs self-hatred. We cling to cheap painted fragments of glass when the pearl of great price is being offered. When a disciple's very existence is threatened, when he stands on the threshold of moral ruin, when everything is at stake, the hour has struck for bold and resolute decision-making. It is not just another itinerant salesperson at the door with superfluous bric-a-brac; it is the Christ of God offering an incredible opportunity, the chance of a lifetime. "I, the light, have come into the world, so that whoever believes in me need not stay in the dark any more" (Jn. 12:46).

In the parable of the talents, the three servants are called to render an account of how they have used the gifts entrusted to them. The first two used their talents boldly and resourcefully. The third, who prudently wraps up his money and buries it, typifies the Christian who deposits his faith in a hermetic container and seals the lid shut. He limps through life on the Baltimore Catechism and resolutely refuses the challenge of growth and spiritual maturity. He wants to take no risks. But precisely because of this, he loses the talent which had been entrusted to him. "The master wanted his servants to take risks. He wanted them to gamble with his money."[6]

In a parable that was undeniably offensive and provocative to his Jewish audience, Jesus told the story of the crafty steward. We are presented with an embezzler who to cover his tracks, launders his employer's money by falsifying his accounts. And Jesus praises the criminal!

"There was a rich man and he had a steward who was denounced to him for being wasteful with his property. He called for the man and said, 'What is this I hear about you? Draw me an account of your stewardship because you are not to be my steward any longer. Then the steward said to himself, 'Now that my master is taking the stewardship from me, what I am to do? Dig? I am not strong enough. Go begging? I should be too ashamed. Ah, I know what I will do to make sure that when I am dismissed from office, there will be some to welcome me into their homes."

Then he called his master's debtors one by one. To the first he said, 'How much do you owe my master?' 'One hundred measures of oil' was the reply. The steward said, 'Here, take your bond; sit down straight away and write fifty'. To another he said, 'And you, sir, how much do you owe?' 'One hundred measures of wheat' was the reply. The steward said, 'Here, take your bond and write eighty.'

The master praised the dishonest steward for his astuteness. For the children of this world are more astute in dealing with their own kind than are the children of light."   (Lk. 16:1-8)

The crafty steward is praised not for his dishonesty but for his astuteness. Jesus does not excuse his action but admires his initiative. He did not let a tragic sequence of events unfold but did what he had to do, however unscrupulously, to make a new life for himself. Without illusions, he makes the most of the little time that remains. "The unjust steward who, hearing he is going to be fired, doctors his master's accounts to secure another job is commended precisely because he acted. The point does not concern morality but apathy. Here is a man who finds himself in a crisis and, instead of wallowing in self-pity, acts resourcefully. The guests who do not respond to the King's banquet are quickly rejected and others are summoned. Immediate response is the mood of the Kingdom. Imaginative shock issues an invitation which leads to decision and action."[7]

The tendency to procrastinate is so prevalent in human beings that it can properly be called an integral part of the human condition. We postpone a decision (which is a decision itself) hoping that the Storyteller will grow weary of waiting and the imperious inner voice will get laryngitis. The call of the parables remains suspended in a state of floating anxiety, so long as we opt neither for or against the new dimension of living opened up to us. The substitute itself creates more problems than it solves and raises again the ominous specter of self-hatred. Procrastination means that we stop growing for an undetermined length of time; we get stuck. And with the paralysis of analysis, the human spirit begins to shrivel. The conscious awareness of our resistance to grace and the refusal to become who we really are brings a sense of oppression. Our lives become fragmented, inconsistent, lacking in harmony and out of sync. The worm turns. The apparent security of staying fixed in a familiar place vanishes. Secretly we long for self-transcendence, for a generosity that would lift us above ourselves. We are caught between a rock and a hard place.

How do we resolve this conundrum? We don't. "Perhaps the best that we can say is that while we cannot will ourselves to grace, we can by will open ourselves to its miraculous coming. We can prepare ourselves to be fertile ground, a welcoming place."[8] There are no magic words, preset formulas or esoteric rites of passage to the grace of self-surrender. Only Jesus Christ delivers us from indecision. The Scriptures offer no other basis for ongoing conversion than the personal magnetism of the Master.

Like any good teacher Jesus frequently repeats himself. He never tires of speaking of the quality of life in the Kingdom and the surpassing joy of the Reign of God:

> "The kingdom of heaven is like a treasure hidden in a field which someone has found; he hides it again, goes off happy, sells everything he owns and buys the field. Again the kingdom of heaven is like a merchant looking for fine pearls; when he finds one of great value he goes and sells everything he owns and buys it. (Mt. 13:44-46)

The emphasis in these parables, as Jeremias insists, is neither the cost of discipleship nor a heartless call to heroic action. The twin stories focus on two unmistakable elements: the joy and delight of discovering the Kingdom of God. Tomorrow if you were notified that you had just won the state lottery — $50,000 per year for the next twenty years — there would be no mumbling, grumbling or complaining about the cruel vicissitudes of life. The only natural response would be sheer delight, delirious joy at the intoxicating prospect of a whole new way of life. The treasure-tracker and the pearl-finder bubble with happiness over their serendipitous stroke of fortune. "When that great joy, surpassing all measure, seizes a man, it carries him away, penetrates his inmost being, subjugates his mind. All else seems valueless compared with that surpassing worth. No price is too great to pay. The unreserved surrender of what is most valuable becomes a matter of course. The decisive thing in the twin parable is not what the two men give up, but their reason for doing so; the overwhelming experience of the splendour of their discovery. Thus it is with the Kingdom of God. The effect of the joyful news is overpowering; it fills the heart with gladness; it makes life's whole aim the consummation of the divine community and produces the most whole-hearted self-sacrifice."⁹

Nevertheless, our own human experience tells us that the Christian life is not lived to a lyrical beat. Precious and few are those moments of boundless delight and delirious joy. Our personal response to the Storyteller is often halting and half-hearted at best. Because the mystery of iniquity lurks on the landscape and the power of sin waxes strong within us, we may come to the Lord bucking, screaming and kicking. The old man dies a slow death; the resistance to the Spirit remains real. The readiness to relinquish everything is more a painful process than a mystical zap. "We are accustomed to imagining the experience of conversion or sudden call to grace as an 'Oh, joy!' phenomenon. In my experience, "We are accustomed to imagining the experience of conversion or sudden call to grace as an 'Oh joy!' phenomenon. In my experience . . . at the moment we finally listen to the call we may say, 'O thank you, Lord'; or we may say, 'O Lord, I am not worthy'; or we may say, 'O Lord, do I have to?'"[10]

Yet, how often have we heard a person say, "Once I finally made up my mind, I found peace." Jesus, who flinched, talked back and questioned God but still remained faithful, reads the human heart and fully understands the nagging uneasiness and subtle self-hatred induced by procrastination. The Story-teller aims to set us free from fence-straddling through the re-telling of the crisis parables. Perhaps their spirit can be illustrated by a story of my own:

"Once there was a certain lawyer named Christopher who lived in Jericho, Long Island. When offered the opportunity of a lucrative partnership in Jerusalem, Pennsylvania, he accepted. Uprooting and transplanting the family was a delicate matter. Two of the children were still in high school and the youngest in the third grade. Nonetheless career advancement, prestige, higher income and a lower cost of living beckoned. Besides, Christopher reasoned, this will be a new beginning. I can start all over.

How badly he wanted that. His drinking was now out of control. The blackouts, the morning bracer and solitary drinking had cunningly crept into his life, almost involuntarily, he felt. How many nights had he slept on the cot in the office after having what he euphemistically called a drink — a 32-ounce bottle of Scotch. His temper tantrums with his secretary were inexcusable. He knew that. Still, it was the pain in Katie's eyes that brought tears to his own. He knew his wife loved him but to learn that she had gone to an Alanon meeting last night . . . Well, all that was behind him. Jerusalem would mark the end of the heyday of the booze, the binges and the bad blood. Jesus, he recalled, had done some memorable things in the biblical town of the same name. So would he.

Christopher did not know that he was destined to die in Jerusalem.

The family moved and he stopped drinking. Cold turkey. The withdrawal had been excruciating — nausea, vomiting, diarrhea, twitching, hallucinations and finally convulsions. Katie saved his life that night. Her husband was a man of exquisite sensitivity and fierce independence. The combination allowed Christopher to defeat John Barleycorn with an iron fist in a velvet glove. All it took was will power, he daily reminded himself. Six weeks of abstinence followed — forty-two full days.

Then his senior partner absconded with the funds, certificates and stocks — bell, book and candle. The law firm collapsed in bankruptcy. Christopher regrouped with a double Scotch straight up. The physical compulsion and mental obsession had returned. The next two months were unadulterated hell. The children withdrew, Katie cried herself to sleep and Christopher drank himself into oblivion. His lights were out, his clock was cleaned, and there was mourning and wailing throughout Jerusalem.

On a Wednesday morning Katie said, "Chris, don't forget your appointment at noon."

"What appointment?"

"Remember, you called Alcoholics Anonymous last night and asked for help."

"Like hell I did!" Another blackout. He remembered John Chancellor on the evening news but after that . . .

The doorbell rang. "I'm Harvey from AA. Your husband called."

Christopher escaped into the kitchen. She pursued him. "Honey, what do you have to lose? Talk with the man."

Beer in hand, he walked into the living room. "Yes, what would you like to talk about?"

"If you put down that can, I'd like to propose a new way of life to you."

For the next two hours Chris endured the drunkalogue as Harvey shared what his life as an alcoholic had been, what happened and what it was now. Grudgingly Chris identified with much of the story. But finally he said, "Thank you. I appreciate what you have had to say. My wife is right. I have abused the gift of the grape. I'll start today to cut down. Goodbye." Christopher vowed to himself that he would not take another drink until eight p.m.

Sipping slowly and triumphantly on that long awaited Scotch, he overheard his wife and eight-year-old son talking in the bedroom. "Vince, why don't you and the other kids play in the pool any more?" The boy hesitated. "I guess I'm frightened. I never know what Dad will be like and I don't want the other boys to see him."

The drink crashed to the floor. Tears cascaded down his cheeks. "Christ, what am I doing? What am I missing?"

Christopher arose from his chair and walked out the door into a new way of life.

Jesus comes to us in the Harveys of our lives, in the destructiveness of the prevailing situation and calls us from despair to hope, from slavery to freedom, from devastating ordinariness to a new way of life. His parables are gifts, shattering our complacency, opening up undreamed of possibilities, promising that we shall have life and have it in abundance. The imaginative shock of his stories make theology by comparison "very old ice cream, very tame sausage."[11]

In our cynical, disillusioned world, we may ask, Is this promise of a new way of life merely an illusion, a figment of the imagination? Let us make a critical distinction: illusion is a denial of reality; imagination creates and calls forth new reality that has not yet come to birth.

Footnotes

[1] *What Are They Saying About Jesus,* Gerald O'Collins, S.J. Paulist Press, N.Y., N.Y. 1977. p. 61. The author quotes Malcolm Muggeridge.

[2] *Jesus — A Gospel Portrait,* Donald Senior, C.P. Ibid. p. 104.

[3] *The Parables of Jesus,* J. Jeremias. Ibid. p. 146.

[4] *Ibid.* p. 163.

[5] *Ibid.* p. 188.

[6] *The Beatitudes: Soundings in Christian Traditions,* Simon Tugwell. Templegate Publishers, Springfield, Il. 1980. p. 23.

[7] *Stories of God,* John Shea. Thomas More Press, Chicago, Il. 1978. p. 187.

[8] *The Road Less Travelled,* M. Scott Peck, M.D. Simon and Schuster, N.Y., N.Y. 1978. p. 308.

[9] Jeremias. *Ibid.* p. 201.

[10] Beck, *Ibid.* p. 305.

[11] Shea. *Ibid.* The author quotes the poet Lawrence Durell. p. 163.

FIVE

LIBERATION THROUGH PRAYER

Whatever else it may be, prayer is first and foremost an act of love. Before any pragmatic, utilitarian or altruistic motivations, prayer is borne of a desire to-be-with the gentlest, most attractive, most interesting and most lovable person I have ever encountered. To really love someone implies a natural longing for presence and intimate communion.

A saint might be simply defined as an extravagant lover of God and people. In the Roman rite, the first scrutiny in the canonization process seeks to establish whether the candidate lived a life of *extraordinary* prayer. Miracles, charismatic gifts and evangelical impact notwithstanding, the cause is dismissed and the candidate disqualified if this criterion of extravagant love of God manifested through heroic prayer is not verified.

Primarily Jesus prayed because he loved his Father. Praise, adoration, thanksgiving, intercession and petition emanated from a profound consciousness of being bonded to the transcendent God in filial intimacy. His personal experience of Yahweh Sabaoth as loving Father shaped not only his self-understanding but, like a knife slashing through wall paper, brought a dramatic breakthrough into undreamed of intimacy with God in prayer. Childlike candor, boundless trust, easy familiarity, deep reverence, joyful dependence, unflagging obedience, unmistakable tenderness and an innate sense of belonging characterized Jesus' prayer.

Basil Pennington, O.C.S.O., captures this simplicity when he writes: "A father is delighted when his little one, leaving off his toys and friends, runs to him and climbs into his arms. As he holds his little one close to him, he cares little whether the child is looking around, his attention flitting from one thing to another, or if he is intent upon his father, or just settling down to sleep. Essentially the child is choosing to be with his father, confident of the love, the care, the security, that is his in those arms. Our Centering Prayer is much like that. We settle down in our Father's arms, in his loving hands. Our mind, our thoughts, our imagination may flit about here and there; we might even fall asleep; but essentially we are choosing to remain for this time intimately with our Father, giving ourselves to him, receiving his love and care, letting him enjoy us as he will. It is very simple prayer. It is very childlike prayer. It is prayer that opens out to us all the delights of the Kingdom."[1]

Through water and the spirit the disciple of Jesus has been bonded to his elder Brother, entered into God's family, become a son of the new Covenant, and given immediate access to the Father's lap. "Blessed be the God and Father of our Lord Jesus Christ . . . Before the world was made, he chose us in Christ, to be holy and spotless, and to live through love in his presence, determining that we should become his adopted sons, through Jesus Christ" (Ep. 1:3-4).

The problem is: either we don't know it, we know it but don't accept it; we accept it but are not in touch with it; we are in touch with it but do not surrender to it.

Self-hatred is not a spiritual sickness that I divined to justify the writing of another book. In my pastoral experience, it is the dominant malaise crippling Christian people and stifling their growth in the Holy Spirit. The National Guild of Catholic Psychiatrists recently reported[2] on the widespread phenomenon of clients tormented by intense feelings of guilt, shame, remorse and self-punishment. The melancholy spirit of Chekhov's plays, "you are living badly, my friend," haunts the American conscience. The disparity between our ideal and real self, the grim spectre of past infidelities, the awareness that I'm not living what I believe, that I am not all that I ought to be, that I am not measuring up to others' expectations of demeanor and lifestyle, the relentless pressure of conformity, the midlife oppression of what I had hoped to become and what I have actually become, the obsession with personal dishonesty and self-centeredness, and our mournful nostalgia for the Blue Lagoon transform an expectant pilgrim people into a dispirited traveling troupe of brooding Hamlets, frightened Rullers and wiped-out Willie Lomans.

Alcoholism, workaholism, mounting addictive behaviors across the board and the alarming suicide rate indicate the magnitude of the problem.

In the struggle with self-hatred, we obviously do not like what we see. It is uncomfortable, if not intolerable, to confront our true selves, and so, like runaway slaves, we either flee our own reality or manufacture a false self which is mostly admirable, mildly prepossessing and superficially happy. Defense mechanisms become useful allies here. These unconscious ploys warp our perception of reality and protect us from fear, loss and emotional pain. Through the smokescreen of rationalization, projection, displacement, insulation, intellectualization and generalization, we remain on the merry-go-round of denial and dishonesty. Those of us who have played this game wear a thousand masks to disguise the face of fear.

Henri Nouwen writes: "There is so much fear in us. Fear of people, fear of God and much raw, undefined, free-floating anxiety. I wonder if fear is not our main obstacle to prayer. When we enter into the presence of God and start to sense the huge reservoir of fear in us, we want to run away into the many distractions which our busy world offers so abundantly. But we should not be afraid of our fears. We can confront them, give words to them and lead them into the presence of him who says, 'Do not be afraid, it is I.' Our inclination is to show the Lord only what we are comfortable with. But the more we dare to reveal our whole trembling self to him, the more we will be able to sense that his love, which is perfect love, casts out all our fears."[3]

To pray is to 'return to ourselves', where God dwells, and accept ownership of our sinfulness, poverty and powerlessness. Only when the prodigal son returned to himself and took inventory of his desperate plight did he begin the journey home to his father. "One of the reasons why our meditation never gets started," wrote the late Thomas Merton, "is that perhaps we never make this real serious return to the center of our own nothingness before God. Hence we never enter into the deepest reality of our relationship with him."[4]

The Lord hears the cry of the poor. When the armistice with self-hatred is signed and we embrace what we really are, the process of liberation begins. But so often we are afraid to do so because of the fear of rejection. Like Quasimodo, the hunchback of Notre Dame who thought he was hideous, we daub cosmetics and spiritual make-up on our misery and supposed ugliness to make ourselves appear presentable to God. This is not our true self. Authentic prayer calls us to rigorous honesty, to come out of hiding, to quit trying to seem impressive, to acknowledge our total dependence on God and the reality of our sinful situation. It is a moment of truth when defenses fall and the masks drop in an instinctive act of humility.

This eleventh hour opening of consciousness has been observed in mental hospitals where mute patients, faced with the reality of the impending showdown, have suddenly begun to speak with passionate conviction about their lives. The prospect of imminent death occasionally has loosened their tongues in the urgent awareness that having lost so much already, they have nothing further to lose through repression and silence.

"Blessed are those who know that they are poor" (NEB). We must know who we are. How difficult it is to be honest — to accept that I am unacceptable, to renounce self-justification, to give up my preposterous pretending that my paltry prayers, spiritual insights, knowledge of Scripture and blustering successes in ministry have made me pleasing to God. No antecedent beauty enamors me in his eyes. I am lovable because He loves me. Period. The first step in liberation from self-hatred is to move from the darkness of self-delusion into the daylight of God's truth.

"We must learn the art of weakness," writes Simon Tugwell, O.P., "of non-achievement, of being able to cope with the knowledge of our own poverty and helplessness, without trying to escape from it into something we can accept more easily. And we must know that it is even in that poverty and helplessness that God sees us with love, even with approbation, however much it may be tinged with regret and censure. God never says to us, 'I want you to be something else' without also saying, 'I love you as you are.'"

Repetitive as it may sound, the Christ of my interiority calls me back tirelessly and insistently to the primordial truth of his unconditional love. His Good News is proclaimed to what we really are, whether we like it or not. Yet the debilitating effects of personal sin make for monstrous resistance to accepting acceptance. A darkened intellect, a weakened will and a panoply of jaded emotions are the stony soil into which the Word of God falls.

From years of clinical practice, the psychiatrist M. Scott Beck, M.D. has come not only to believe in original sin; he has given it a precise definition — *laziness.* Prayer becomes a chore rather than a joy. The confessor is obliged to say, "For your penance, pray three Our Fathers." We drag ourselves out of bed for morning praise, shuffle off to liturgy with the sacramental slump of the terminally ill, get a reprieve with "the Mass is ended, go in peace," and endure the tedium of night prayer with stoic resignation knowing that "this too shall pass." The Enemy, who specializes in treacherous disguise, is the lazy part of self that is resisting the effort, asceticism and discipline that a serious life of prayer demands. The faulty logic of a darkened intellect permits dubious rationalizations such as, "my work is my prayer; I'm too busy, I only pray when I feel a prompting of the Spirit." These lame excuses allow us lazily to maintain the status quo and indefinitely postpone the tryst with unconditional love.

Moreover, the quid pro quo character of human love with its inevitable disillusionments and disappointments unconsciously becomes operative in the divine encounter and impedes the inbreak into Mystery. The lived experience of gratuitous love that knows no boundary, limit or breaking point is a *rara avis,* even in honeymoon havens like Bali Hai or the Poconos.

But what if it should come to pass?

Again, laziness, manifested as fear of the sweat and struggle involved in spiritual growth, intrudes. God loves me as I am, but he loves me so much that he won't let me stay where I am. Where does the road lead? The dread of journeying into the unknown, the uneasiness of knowing that the Holy One will not be manipulated, that he cannot be conned into granting consolation when he is calling for conversion, that accepting unconditional love leads to loving unconditionally in return — these stumbling blocks discourage every prodigal from returning to himself. Their names are laziness and fear.

Anyone who walks in alcoholic bones is no stranger to self-deception. He steps gingerly through the minefield of dishonesty and deceit knowing that his very life hangs in the balance. No one has ever intellectualized himself into sobriety (I sure as hell haven't), just as no one intellectualizes himself into prayer. Recognition of the problem is not the answer. Action is. One learns to pray by praying.

Forty minutes of prime time in solitary prayer, usually divided into two twenty-minute periods, before a symbol of the crucified Christ is the most effective discipline I have found for making conscious contact with the living God and his liberating love. Lamentably, Christian piety has prettified the passionate God of Golgotha; Christian art has banalized unspeakable outrage into dignified jewelry; Christian worship has sentimentalized monstrous scandal into sacred pageant. We have corrupted our sense of reality by sentimentalizing it. Pious imagination, romantic preaching and lifeless or raucous worship overshadow the real Jesus. The Christian should tremble and the whole community quake during the veneration of the cross on Good Friday. But organized religion has domesticated the crucified Lord of glory into a tame theological symbol. He does not disturb our comfortable piety. Yet, all the heretics, ayatollahs and flamboyant pentecostal preachers put together create less havoc than the Crucified when "instead of remaining an icon, he comes to life and delivers us over to the fire that he came to light."[6]

For the believing Christian, prayer before a crucifix exposes skepticism as academia, cynicism as a loss of nerve and indifference as downright bad faith. The crucified Christ, now risen in glory, is not an abstraction but the ultimate response to how far love will go, what measure of rejection it will endure, how much infidelity, self-centeredness and betrayal it will withstand. The unconditional love of Jesus Christ nailed to the wood does not flinch before the worst sinner's perversity and inhumanity. "He took our sicknesses away and carried our diseases for us" (Mt. 8:17).

The Christ of Christian prayer is the risen One

who still bears the nailmarks of the earthly Jesus, without which he would not be identical with the Nazarene. "Harsh though it may sound, it is obvious that Christ is denied today by Christians most of all, because his lordship over their organized religion and their dogmatic convictions has become illusory, theoretical and imaginary. But the token which distinguishes his lordship from the lordship of other religious founders is undoubtedly the cross and the cross alone."[7]

Our presence to him in prayer can accomplish nothing of itself but it does create the situation where he may speak to us through his Spirit if he wishes, enlighten our minds with his wisdom, and liberate us from self-hatred if he deems it opportune. Here I would like to share an exercise that I have found profitable for experiencing the love of Jesus Christ:

I learnt this from an evangelical pastor who seemed to have the gift for mediating the experience of Jesus Christ, the risen Lord, to people who asked to come in touch with Christ. As nearly as I can remember the pastor's words, his method was something like this:

Let us suppose someone came to him and said, 'I want to come in touch with the risen Lord.' The pastor would lead him to a quiet corner. They would both close their eyes and bow their heads in prayer.

The pastor would then say something like this to the other person: 'Listen carefully to what I have to say now: Jesus Christ, the risen Lord, is present here and now with us. Do you believe this?' After a pause the man would say, 'Yes, I believe it.'

"Now I am going to get you to consider something that is even more difficult to believe. Jesus Christ, the risen Lord who is present here, loves and accepts you just as you are . . . You do not have to change to get his love . . . You do not have to become better . . . to get out of your sinful ways . . . He obviously wants you to become better. He obviously wants you to give up your sin. But you do not have to do this to get his love and acceptance. That you have already, right now, just as you are, even before you decide to change, and whether you decide to change or not . . . Do you believe this? . . . Take your time over it . . . Then decide whether you believe it or not."

After some reflection the man would say, "Yes, I believe that, too."

"Well, then," says the pastor, "Say something to Jesus. Say it aloud."

The man begins to pray aloud to the Lord . . . and it isn't long before he grasps the pastor's hand and says, 'I know exactly what you mean about experiencing him. He is here! I can sense his presence.'

Sheer imagination? A special charism given to our good pastor? Perhaps. The fact is that, whether or not this method is adequate for putting a person in contact with the risen Lord it is certainly a sound one and the method certainly conducive to making a person feel the infinite treasures of the love of Christ. Try it for yourself:

Recall the presence of the risen Lord with you . . . Tell him you believe that he is present to you . . .

Reflect on the fact that he loves and accepts you just as you are now . . . Take time out to sense his unconditional love for you as he looks at you *lovingly and humbly.*

Speak to Christ . . . or just lovingly stay in silence and communicate with him beyond words.

The devotion to the Heart of Christ, so vigorous

some years ago, so much on the decline today, would flourish once again if people would understand that it consists essentially in accepting Jesus Christ as love incarnate, as the manifestation of the unconditional love of God for us. Anyone who accepts this is bound to experience fruits *beyond all his expectations* in his own prayer life and in his ministry. "The great turning point in your life comes not when you realize that you love God but when you realize and fully accept the fact that God loves you unconditionally."[8]

Liberation from Time

Neither my seminary training, the Second Vatican Council nor my last thirty-day retreat prepared me for the news, but some well-informed sources recently reported that the end of the world is imminent. Though Jesus himself disclaimed any knowledge of the day or the hour (Mt. 24:36), these visionaries have assured us that the nuclear impasse is at the brink, the global village is teetering on the edge, and very soon things will be all over for the human adventure.

The seers may be correct in their apocalyptic ultimatum — that human history has come to an end and the extermination of the species is at hand. The evils of the present generation may indeed be interpreted as signs signalling God's final intervention to bring about the end-time in awesome destruction and incredible triumph. On the other hand, they may be completely mistaken.

Dr. James Mackey writes: "Apocalyptic holds a certain morbid fascination for the human mind. It easily outlives the circumstances which give it birth, and always finds groups to predict the end of the world over the graves of all former predictions. Symbols are always vulnerable to over-literal minds and the inflated images of apocalyptic seem more prone than most to be taken literally. But the tendency to take apocalyptic too literally is due to a disease of the human mind rather than to any inherent fault in apocalyptic itself. It is due to a failure of nerve, to the hypochondriac's penchant for exaggerating the evils of the age, and to the coward's anxious search for an escape clause in humanity's contract with history."[9]

In either event, the Lordship of Jesus Christ extends over the cosmic continuum. "I am the Alpha and the Omega, the First and the Last, the Beginning and the End" (Rv. 22:13). Authentic prayer puts us in touch with this reality and liberates us from the tyranny of time. His word calls us to conscientious conduct in the world day; tomorrow's survival is his responsibility.

The New Testament knows only the linear concept of time. Creation marked the beginning, the death/resurrection of Christ was the decisive midpoint, and his Second Coming determines the endtime. But this latter future event is no longer the center of redemptive history. Regardless of the precise date of the Parousia, we are living in the last days or in Oscar Cullman's oft-quoted phrase, in "the isness of the shall be."[10] The final stage of salvation-history was inaugurated on Easter Sunday. By way of illustration: many historians see the battle of Iwo Jima as the turning point of World War II in the South Pacific. This decisive victory so close to the heart of the Japanese mainland was achieved; yet the war still continued. Though the significance of the flag-raising on Iwo was not fully perceived by all, it nevertheless made eventual conquest of the Japanese inevitable. But the war was still carried on for an undefined time, until "VJ Day." In the Christian view of history the end-time is coming, but the world is already ruled by Christ by virtue of his decisive Paschal victory.

Several times a day most people will glance at their watch or the wallclock or ask, "What time is it?" To our earth-bound minds Jesus whispers in prayer: *"Now* is the time! The 'real' world of price tags, who shot J.R., Gucci handbags, monopoly money, the iron umbrella of nuclear deterrence, beaver vests, Persian rugs, silk underwear and Super Bowl LXXVII, is passing away. *Now* is the time to stop running around frantically like Lancelot's horse in four directions at once and quietly remember that only one thing is necessary. *Now* is the time for creative response to my Word and saving solutions for your brothers and sisters. Let me tell you a little story: One year a rich fool had a bonanza crop and made provisions for a yet heavier one. He said to himself, 'You're a good ole boy. You've worked hard, deserve everything that's coming to you, and have a nestegg for the future. Take it easy, eat heartily, drink up a storm and have a good time.'

"That night my Father shattered his security. 'Fool! This very night the demand will be made for your soul; and this hoard of yours, who is going to enjoy it now?'"

In prayer Jesus slows us down to a human tempo, teaches us to count how few days we have, gifts us with wisdom of heart, and liberates us from the oppression of false deadlines, myopic vision and the degradation of language. (With reference to the latter, I have discovered that prayer has purified my vocabulary of many boring, colorless, puffy and apparently damned important words like maximize, prioritize, interact, facilitate, interface, input, feedback and bottomline. There is a conspicuous absence of empty, overused words in Jesus' speech. We find no trace of impacting, hopefully, at this point in time, parameters or linkages in the Gospel; in fact there are no junk words, jargon or *meaningful* nonsense at all.)

Sir Thomas More, a man for all seasons, is my candidate for the patron saint of the 1980's. His marvelous sense of humor evolved from his concept of linear time, a lucid, sensible appreciation of death and the folly of this transitory world. More's life was anchored in Jesus Christ, the Alpha and Omega who rules as Lord over all things in heaven and on earth. In his world-view it had already been drawn inexorably into the redemptive process. No power or principality could prevail against Christ's Lordship over time. God had destined More's world for good, and in spite of the most fearful indications to the contrary, good would triumph because Jesus had already accomplished the victory.

The saint saw through the make-believe character of this world and could not stop laughing at human conceit. "So clear was his intuitive vision of the Eternal that he could only see life in this world from God's point of view. So much of what he saw looked so very much like play acting that he could not take it seriously."[11]

Husband, father, prominent statesman, author, a political man of his times, More was nonetheless a true contemplative who lived an extraordinary life of prayer. "His is, in a sense, the superb example of a man whose sense of humour stemmed from his prayer and mirrored his love of God. Seeing this life as a stage and all the men and women merely players, he could only see the funny side of human conceit."[12] With notable exceptions, most of the canonized saints seem to be otherworldly and grim, if not forbidding. The gaunt ascetic who practices heroic self-denial may take a dim view of the world and human relationships. The apostolic workaholic may give the impression that he has mislaid true peace and joy. The Spartan who is merciless with himself may incline to be unbending with others. Thomas More was a charming, delightful and witty man who was in the world and of the world, attached to the city and devoted to the temple. His life of prayer preserved the delicate balance in fruitful tension.

In our own era, when the false claims of Madison Avenue brainwashing work to seduce the human spirit and persuade us that happiness lies in the swirling caress of an onyx jacuzzi, More's realism and mordant wit are timely, sobering and benignly outrageous. His revolt against unreality and his ruthless rejection of humbug put time and its trappings in biblical perspective.

His most hilarious barbs were reserved for kings and clergy, talkative nuns and inflated theologians and one Elmer Gantry-like character called Candidus, a parish priest who was a dubious model of Christian discipleship:

"As a faithful mirror view it,
Showing what to do — what shun;
All he shuns take care to do it,
All he does, take care to shun."[13]

It would not have been uncharacteristic of More to lampoon contemporary theology in the style of this anonymous wit: "Jesus said to his disciples, 'Who do men say that I am?' And they answered him: You are the eschatological manifestation of the ground of our being, in whom we find the ultimate fulfillment in our interpersonal relationships.' And Jesus said: 'What?'"

Yet, for all More's witty and savage attacks on the Establishment, his prayer-life exerted a decisive influence on his political thought, political passion and political action. The Chancellor of England did not run from the world but to it in Christ Jesus. He got deeply involved in British trade agreements and labor negotiations, championed the rights of the poor and oppressed who were being used as cattle, waged war on high prices and the shortage of food, bitterly opposed the bellicose political stance of several popes, urged the reform of law and the spread of scholarship, and became so embroiled in his own personal declaration of religious freedom that it led to his martyrdom at the hands of King Henry VIII in 1535.

Liberated through prayer from the tyranny of time, More could proclaim unpretentiously, "The King's good servant but God's first." Alas, his sense of humor did not desert him even on the scaffold. As the executioner raised high the axe, More implored that his beard be spared from the block "for this has committed no treason."[14]

The patron saint for the American Church in the 1980's? Why not? In the year 1929, the late G. K. Chesterton prophesied: "Sir Thomas More is more important at this moment than at any moment since his death, even perhaps the great moment of his dying; but he is not quite so important as he will be in a hundred years time."[15]

In Morris West's most recent novel, *The Clowns of God,* the inherent tensions of Christian eschatology are explored through the fictional character of Pope Gregory XVII. Forced to abdicate the papacy because he claims to have received *in prayer* a private revelation of the end of the world and the Second Coming of Christ, the pontiff is deposed and exiled by the college of cardinals for not playing with a full deck. His mystical experience has radically altered his concept of time and given birth to a new agenda, a different set of priorities and a prophetic vision of Church. While the well-oiled machinery of Vatican diplomacy and Roman bureaucracy continues to clack at staccato pace, Gregory agonizes night and day over the nightmare of imminent nuclear escalation that will precipitate the Parousia.

In his mind "everything else became petty and irrelevant: dogmatic disputes, some poor priest hopping into bed with a housemaid, whether a woman should take a little pill or carry a little card to count her lunar periods to avoid making gunfodder for the day of Armageddon . . . "[16]

With a live grenade ticking in the background, Gregory's Church has no more urgent priority than proclaiming Jesus, preparing the way for him, and not getting panic-stricken when he appears on the scene. It is neither to get bogged down in heresy hunting nor mired in the ecclesiastical morass of theological controversies. With precious time slipping away like sand in an hour-glass, the Church must preach from the rooftops that Jesus Christ is saving Lord, at least let people hear and respond to his life-giving question to Peter, "Do you love me?", and allow Jesus' sovereignty to become a reality in the realm of Christian freedom. The qahal Yahweh, the ekklesia, the holy Church of God will call people to renounce mean-minded narrowness and denominational differences, to bond together in little communities who will pray together and heal and serve one another because "the Kingdom of God is a dwelling place for men. What else can it signify but a condition in which human existence is not only tolerable but joyful — because it is open to infinity."[17]

One should not lose sight of this central truth: the earthquake in the life of More's fictional hero occurred in the purifying solitude of prayer. It was not only a liberating and lacerating revelation but a revolutionary one as well. "Jesus Christ is the same yesterday, today and forever" (Heb. 13:8). Why should the experience of liberation from the dominion of self-hatred and the tyranny of time be any different for us?

Footnotes

[1] *Centering Prayer,* Basil Pennington, O.C.S.O. Doubleday & Co. Inc., Garden City, N.Y. 1980. pp. 68-69.

[2] Michael E. Cavanagh, "Understanding Guilt," *Bulletin of the National Guild of Catholic Psychiatrists 23* (1977; pp. 11-18. Quoted in *Guilt — Fifth Psychotheological Symposium.)* Affirmation Books, Whitinsville, MA. 1980. p. 125.

[3] *A Cry For Mercy,* Henri J. M. Nouwen. Doubleday & Co., Garden City, N.Y. 1981. p. 23.

[4] *The Climate of Monastic Prayer,* Thomas Merton. Quoted by Pennington, *Ibid.* p. 73.

[5] *The Beatitudes: Soundings in Christian Traditions,* Simon Tugwell. *Ibid.* p. 15.

[6] *Jesus Means Freedom,* Ernst Kasemann. *Ibid.* p. 150.

[7] *Perspectives on Paul,* E. Kasemann. *Ibid.* p. 54.

[8] *Sadhana — A Way to God,* Anthony de Mello S.J. *Ibid.* pp. 114-116.

[9] *Jesus the Man and the Myth,* James P. Mackey. *Ibid.* p. 126.

[10] *Christ and Time,* Oscar Cullman. Westminster Press, Philadelphia, PA. 19107. p. 84. The author's insight into the primitive Christian conception of time and history is the basis for my reflection.

[11] *Born For Friendship, The Spirit of Sir Thomas More,* Bernard Bassett, S.J., Sheed and Ward, N.Y. 1965. p. 40.

[12] *Ibid.* p. 43.

[13] *Ibid.* p. 41.

[14] *Ibid.* p. 211.

[15] *The Fame of Blessed Thomas More,* G. K. Chesterton, Sheed and Ward, 1929, p. 63. Quoted by Bassett in his Foreword.

[16] *The Clowns of God,* Morris West. William Morrow and Company, New York. 1981. p. 112.

[17] *Ibid.* p. 253.

SIX

INTEGRITY AND SELF-ACCEPTANCE

On an overcast spring morning in 1979, four Christians of varying intensity were strolling through the French Quarter in New Orleans. It was a contrived celebration, a plotted playday, a deliberate and mischievous escape from the weary round of work. The hour was gliding toward noon. We passed Al Hirt's jazz emporium, browsed in a homely boutique to sniff scented candles and ambled on to Jackson Square. The Court of the Two Sisters featured red beans and rice for its luncheon fare. A trifling temptation. We were moving in para-liturgical procession to Pontalba's, the home of the muffalletta. My face was set like flint. Paul's eyes narrowed with the apocalyptic glint of an aimed gun. Salivating in greedy anticipation of the first bite — Genoa salami, provolone, diced olives, bologna and prosciutto laced with a bewitching sauce and wedged within a cavernous sesame bun, we sat down at a circular marble table.

Paul turned to me and asked, "What do you want to do with the rest of your life?" With only slight hesitation I replied, "I would like the epitaph on my tombstone to read, "Here lies a loving man.""

Even when preoccupied, distracted or salivating, we each have a dream, a vision of life that corresponds to our convictions, embodies our uniqueness and expresses what is life-giving within us. Whether altruistic or ignoble, the dream gives definition to our lives, influences the decisions we make, the steps we take and the words we speak. If security represents our highest aspirations, we may be owned and indentured by Aetna Life and Casualty; if pleasure is our priority, we will distribute our time and money in hedonistic pursuits; if scholarship rules, we will be properly pedigreed and securely settled in an academic environment. Even if the dream is unrealistic or temporarily on hold due to uncontrollable circumstances, it prods our consciousness, nurtures our fantasies, and inchoatively sustains our will-to-meaning in the world.

The dream of Jesus Christ is the Kingdom of God, and the committed Christian buys into his dream.

It ought to be noted that the Kingdom is not an abstraction. It is a concrete, visible and formidable reality forged by the personal commitment of many members. A commitment that does not issue in humble service, suffering discipleship and creative love is an illusion. The world has no interest in abstractions and Jesus Christ is impatient with illusions. "Everyone who listens to these words of mine and does not act on them will be like a stupid man who built his house on sand" (Mt. 7:26).

"The one who talks, especially if he talks to God, can effect a great deal, but the one who acts really means business and has more claim on our attention. If you want to know what a person really believes, Blondel says somewhere, don't listen to what he says but watch what he does."[1]

A life of integrity is born of fidelity to the dream. Daily we make choices that are either consistent with or contrary to the Gospel vision. The mature Christian has harmoniously integrated his faith, intellect and feelings in consistent and fairly predictable behavioral patterns. The sense of serenity that springs from this internal continuity is self-acceptance. The need for approval and the hunger for human respect diminishes in proportion to our integrity. (The Scriptures call it righteousness, but the word has a pejorative tone in our times, as does piety, and both ought to be scrapped for the duration or until such time as words are restored to their original meaning. They conjure up notions of legalism, spiritual superiority and sanctimonious moralism that would make Jesus shudder).

Each Christian gives flesh and bone to the dream in his own unique, mysterious and irreplaceable personality. The Word of God calls into being a faith-community characterized by unity without uniformity. Jesus is the way, but his light is refracted in myriad ways by multiple personalities. "To be open to the Way, the Truth and the Life, we should find the unique task and expression of divine love Jesus wants in our lives. In countless loving and caring ways, we can put ourselves in our daily tasks and encounters, but only one way can build the style of divine caring each one of us is uniquely called to by the Lord. There are many tempting possibilities to care in ways that are at odds with the way Christ wants to express care in us. We may try to live a style of love we are not called to. We may want to concretize our care for people in a task or movement not attuned to our individual nature. We may do so to please others because we crave to be liked. Or we may want to belong to a popular social or apostolic movement. We join in blindly in spite of the fact that their particular manifestation of Christ's love is not necessarily ours."[2]

Discerning the direction that the dream should take in our lives requires fidelity to our feelings. Emotions, mistrusted and much maligned in the checkered history of Christian spirituality, are integral parts of our total self. They are the most direct reaction to our perception of ourselves and the world around us. Whether positive or negative, feelings put us in touch with our true selves. They are neither good nor bad; they are simply the truth of what is going on within us. What we do with them will determine whether we live lives of honesty or deceit. The familiar reproach, "You lied to me," is often valid even when we have told the truth. The other only heard what we said but not what we meant because we repressed our feelings. When submitted to the discretion of a faith-formed intellect, our emotions serve as accurate and trustworthy beacons for appropriate action or inaction.

Feelings that are not expressed cannot be fixed. For example, suppressed anger leads to resentment; repressed resentment leads to guilty self-flagellation; guilt leads to depression. Repressed persons are often depressed persons. An integral life implies creative listening to our emotions, taking responsibility for them and courageously expressing them. The denial, displacement or suppression of feelings constitutes infidelity to the dream and leads to a loss of integrity.

Three years ago, a quintet of computer salesmen from Milwaukee went to a regional sales convention in Chicago. They assured their wives that they would return in ample time for dinner. The meeting ran overtime, and the men raced to the train station

tickets in hand. As they barged through the terminal,
one man inadvertently kicked over a table supporting
a basket of apples. Without stopping, they reached
the train and boarded it with a sign of relief. All but
one. He paused, got in touch with his feelings, and
experienced a twinge of compunction for the boy
whose applestand had been overturned. He waved
goodbye to his companions and returned to the
terminal. He was glad he did. The ten-year-old boy
was blind.

The salesman gathered up the apples and noticed
that several were bruised. He reached in his pocket
and said to the child, "Please accept ten dollars for the
damage we did. I hope it didn't spoil your day." As he
started to walk away, the bewildered little boy called
after him, "Are you Jesus?"

To ignore, repress or be inattentive to our
feelings is to fail to listen to the stirrings and surprises
of the Spirit within our emotional structure calling us
to creative response.

Jesus listened. In John's gospel we are told that
"he was moved with the deepest emotions" (11:33). In
Matthew his anger erupts: "You hypocrites! It was
you Isaiah meant when he prophesied: This people
honors me only with lip-service, while their hearts are
far from me. The worship they offer me is worthless"
(15:7-9). He calls the crowd to intercessory prayer
because "he felt sorry for them because they were
harassed and dejected like sheep without a shepherd
(Mt. 9:16). When the Lord saw the widow of Naim,
"he *felt* sorry for her. 'Don't cry,' he said" (Lk. 7:13).
Would her son have been restored to life if Jesus had
repressed his feelings? Grief, frustration and sadness
spontaneously break through when "he drew near and
came in sight of the city, he shed tears for it and said,

"If you in your turn had only understood the message of peace" (Lk. 19:41). There is no trace of emotional restraint when Jesus roars, "You liars! The devil is your father and you prefer to do what your father wants" (Jn. 8:55, 44). There is more than a hint of irritation when dining at Simon's house in Bethany, he says, "Leave her alone. Why are you upsetting her?" (Mk. 14:6). We hear utter frustration in the words, "How much longer must I put up with you?" (Mt. 15:17), unmitigated rage in, "Get behind me, Satan! You are an obstacle in my path" (Mt. 16:23), extraordinary sensitivity in "Who touched me? I felt that power had gone out from me" (Lk. 8:47), and blazing wrath in, "Get them out of here! Stop turning my Father's house into a marketplace" (Jn. 2:16).

The gospel portrait of Jesus is that of a man exquisitely attuned to his emotions and uninhibited in expressing them. One finds in Christ no attitude of scorn, contempt, fear, ridicule or rejection of feelings as being, fickle, flaky and unreliable. They were sensitive emotional attennae to which he listened carefully and through which he perceived the will of his Father for congruent speech and action. (There is an untapped mine of spiritual wisdom in the soporific slogan, "If it feels good, do it." Admittedly, its meaning has been bent, twisted, spindled and mutilated by hedonists and Epicureans in order to rationalize licentious behavior; nevertheless, good feelings, consonant with our faith-commitment and intellectual perception, are signals for creative Christian conduct fruitful for ourselves, others and the building of the Kingdom).

The light we are seeking is inside. So often we search for God willy-nilly and do not find him until we return to ourselves. In active listening to our feelings we encounter the Holy, not in the earthquake and fire outside, but like Elijah "in the sound of a gentle breeze" (1 Kgs. 19:23). The Kingdom of God is in our midst.

Jesus' freedom from public opinion and the nagging concern of what others might think enabled him to vent his emotions with honesty and spontaneity. There could be no facade, no mask, no pretense, no sham, no playing of roles. For the Nazarene carpenter to have integrity meant to be genuine, to communicate authentically, to resonate with his feelings. On the contrary, to be false, two-faced, to be less than real, to say one thing and mean another was to lose self and deny the dream. "I tell you this, that for every unfounded word men utter they will answer on Judgment Day, since it is by your words you will be acquitted, and by your words condemned" (Mt. 12:36).

A life of integrity is not necessarily a life of conformity. The injunction of Paul to "put on Christ" explicitly means not to conform to the spirit of this passing age. With utter single-mindedness and purity of heart, Jesus sought only to please his Father. He was unconcerned about projecting a "nice guy" image and surely not paranoid about hurting anyone's feelings or stepping on any toes. "There is a kind of tyranny of public opinion which we often find at work in human life, in our own lives: What will the neighbors think! What will my friends think! What will people think! The expectations of others often act as a subtle but controlling pressure on behavior. But the claim of God's Kingdom take precedence over the claims of what others may think, even if that priority is difficult to observe. Because he remains free for the claims of the Kingdom, Jesus is able to maintain a freedom from the narrow judgments of those who would straitjacket him in a conventional mold."[3]

John Haughey S.J., has remarked that the best way for anyone to grow is "to put down roots." Jesus' life was a developing consciousness of his person and his mission through rootedness in his Father. Like a massive oak tree with its roots buried deep in the earth, Jesus' heart was buried in the One whom he affectionately called "Abba" and bonded in love in a way that goes beyond our understanding. He clung to his Father and never camouflaged his feelings, shouted with the crowd or rippled in the wind of pusillinamity and compromise. He knew who he was — the Son, Servant and Beloved of his Father — and he permitted nothing and no one to stand in his way of being himself. "Not the law, not the tradition, not the past, not the authorities, not public opinion, not even death itself. Nothing! He will be the Father's Son, which is the very essence of his identity. He will be himself."[4]

In the full acceptance of who he was Jesus is the archetype of personality integration. When we "put on Christ" and fully accept who we are, a healthy independence from peer pressure, people-pleasing and human respect develops. Christ's preferences and values become our own. The Kingdom of God is built on earth when we do the will of our Father in heaven. We become 'other Christs' through a life of Christian integrity. The same openness to feelings, simplicity of speech, intimacy with the Father, spirit of humble service, compassionate healing, suffering discipleship and obedient love is wrought in us by the Paraclete and precises what Paul means by "new creation."

We ought to humbly underline the title 'other Christs' for nothing less describes the reality. In the pre-conciliar church this dignity was reserved for an elite, a select few of the "holy nation" (1 Pt. 2:9) on the basis of sacramental ordination through the laying on of hands. Nothing is further from the gospel truth. This is a serious injustice to the "royal priesthood" which is *all* the holy people of God. Every Christian who walks in the way of integrity and fidelity to the dream is 'another Christ.' "No human beings are, by virtue of office or state in life, holier or more sacred in their persons or closer to God than others; and whatever sense we may now make of priesthood in the Christian community, we may never again think of priests as 'other Christs' in a sense in which all Christian people cannot be called other Christs, nor can we see them as standing between God and others, mediators between God and humanity. One is the mediator, Jesus, and through him all have immediate access to God. Neither cult nor creed, neither code nor institution, can ever again be allowed to rob people of the conviction conveyed in the mission of Jesus that God is Father to all, present to all in the gift of life and world which he gives to all without distinction, and accessible to all through the lives they live in the world they know."[5]

While the way of integrity offers no grounds for boasting because it is the work of the Spirit within us (and this is no token acknowledgment; without the Holy Spirit we cannot even see that Jesus is risen), it does call the disciple to rigorous honesty about his attitudes, values, lifestyle and personal relationships. In my experience of life on the streets, honesty is a rare and precious quality seldom found in society or in the church. Like the alcoholic who denies he has a drinking problem, many of us have been deluding ourselves for so long, that dishonesty and self-deception have become an accepted way of life. The *esse quam videri* (to be rather than seem to be) of St. Gregory Nazianzen has been so convoluted that 'seeming to be' becomes the common denominator of ordinary behavior, pretense and sham comprise enough to get by, pious thoughts replace putting on an apron and washing dirty feet, and in the words of Carl Jung, "neurosis is always an adequate substitute for suffering."[6]

In my broken days of sour wine and withered roses, when I was stashing Vodka bottles in the bathroom, glove compartment and geranium pot, I presumed that no one suspected and that the One who knows how to play twenty questions was either out to lunch or off to Nairobi. The mind plays tricks. Sober or inebriated, self-deception is a cunning, baffling and powerful enemy of integrity. I have found no simple solution in the struggle for ruthless honesty but, returning to the epitaph on my tombstone, I have begun to pause on the hour to briefly examine whether or not the thoughts, words and deeds of the previous sixty minutes go with the flow of my dream of being a loving man. Should this practice lead to navel-gazing, unhealthy introversion and self-preoccupation, I shall not ask how the jackass got into the ditch but simply work to get him out.

The gradual transformation from an attitude of self-hatred to a spirit of self-acceptance is what occurs in the process of trying to be honest. Paradoxically, the human spirit soars in the daily endeavor to make choices and decisions that are expressive of the truth of who we are in Christ Jesus, not who we think we should be or who somebody else wants us to be. Self-mastery over every form of sin, selfishness, emotional dishonesty and degraded love is the less-travelled road to Christian freedom. "You cannot belong to Christ Jesus unless you crucify all self-indulgent desires and passions" (Ga. 5:24). At the outset, the perfect joy of St. Francis may be an unrealistic expectation, but each small victory over self-indulgence yields its own measure of elation. The beginning of Brother Leo's peptic ulcer probably can be traced to the day that Francis explained to him the meaning of perfect joy: "Above all the graces and gifts of the Holy Spirit which Christ gives to his friends is that of conquering himself and willingly enduring sufferings, insults, humiliations and hardships for the love of Christ." Leaving levity in its place, there is no growth without pain, no integrity without self-denial, and neither particularly attractive apart from the personal love of Jesus Christ.

In the last analysis, the dream is not a way of thinking or a way of speaking but a way of living. Yet, the way of integrity holds no real appeal to me independent of an intimate relationship with Jesus. Self-conquest for its own sake, penitential practices such as fasting and flagellation for self-discipline, and the Spartan lifestyle as an end in itself are for souls braver than I. Unless Jesus enfleshes the dream and inspirits the integrity, it loses its fascination and is stripped of its mystique. When the Crucified says, "I'm dying to be with you," and then whispers, "Will you die a little to be with me?", my sluggish spirit is stirred (unfortunately not always) to prefer the pleasure of his company to whatever trinket of creation is mesmerizing me at the moment.

Thus, the attitude of self-acceptance is not essentially self-centered. It is radically relational. It is not self-regarding but Christ-oriented. The spurious self-contentment that evolves from scrupulous self-examination, rigorous mortification and the anxious endeavor to achieve purity of heart is bogus spirituality, the counterfeit coin of Christian integrity. As Jesus' unparalleled authenticity and inner serenity were rooted in his Father's good pleasure, so Christian self-acceptance is planted is the conscious and experiential affirmation of Jesus in our struggle to be faithful.

A fellow Franciscan once challenged me: "Do you ever reflect upon the fact that Jesus feels proud of you? Proud that you accepted the faith which he offered you? Proud that you chose him for a friend and Lord? Is proud of you that you haven't given up? Proud that you believe in him enough to try again and again? Proud that you trust that he can help you? Do you ever think that Jesus appreciates you for wanting him, for wanting to say no to so many things that would separate you from him? Do you think that Jesus can ever be grateful to you for pausing to smile, comfort, give to one of his children who have such great need to see a smile, to feel a touch? Do you ever think of Jesus being grateful to you for learning more about him so that you can speak to others more deeply and truly about him? Do you ever think that Jesus can be angry or disappointed in you for not believing that he has forgiven you totally? He said, "I do not call you servants, but friends . . . " Therefore, there is the possibility of every feeling and emotion which can exist between friends to exist here and now between Jesus and you."

A wise man once said that a truly intelligent person is one who has learned to be happy with himself. The secret of self-acceptance, often hidden from the wise and clever, the Ph.D.'s and power brokers of this world, is the way of integrity born of fidelity to the dream. When we are comfortable with ourselves, a new-found freedom blossoms. Am I free? If not, why not? The familiar words of the Serenity Prayer: "God, grant me the serenity to accept the things I cannot change, the courage to change the things I can, and the wisdom to know the difference," provoke the question, "What is not working in my life? What am I afraid of losing? What is robbing me of inner peace? What attitude, behavioral pattern or disordered relationship is making me frightened of the face in the mirror? Do I have the courage to change the things I can? The mere willingness to confront the question often unlocks the door to self-acceptance.

"When we accept ourselves for what we are, we cease to hunger for power or the acceptance of others because our self-intimacy reinforces our inner sense of security. We are no longer preoccupied with being powerful or popular. We no longer fear criticism or contradiction because we accept the reality of human limitations. Integrated, we are no longer plagued with the desire to please others because simply being true to ourselves brings lasting inner peace. We accept our feelings as part of ourself. We appreciate and listen to them. Accepting our feelings allows us to choose appropriate behavior patterns that are beneficial to ourselves and others. Personality integration allows us to enjoy life responsibly and to discover the particular meaning of our own particular lives. We are grateful for life and we deeply appreciate and love ourselves."[7]

The risk-taking disciple who dares to listen to his feelings, rather than to the voice of authority or to the majority, may quickly discover that his inner echoes do not resonate with the *vox populi*. He finds that this is unnerving to himself and disturbing to the palace guard. Though Abraham Maslow might describe him as "unique and idiosyncratic, alive and creative rather than inhibited, conventionalized and artificial, honest rather than phony,"[8] the nervous disciple finds little solace in the eulogy. He is pretty damn frightened about swimming upstream. His security blanket of respectability has been snatched away and he wanders temporarily in a Linus-like trance. His coveted image of propriety and sobriety, watchman against novelty and creativity, custodian of the status quo, pillar of orthodoxy and vigilante of the via media is blown to hell by innuendo and mistrust. "The crazy bastard flipped out," says the bartender, and the sages on the stools nod gravely over their grog.

The risk-takers, who listen to the Spirit speaking through their feelings are ready to chance something, fully aware that the history of Christian spirituality is not one of obedient conformity, however much some people prefer to view it that way. Rather, as Francis, Dominic, Ignatius and others saw, it is a history of fidelity to the dream, writing the gospel afresh for one's own generation, and imaginative response to the needs of the Church. Their dream, insofar as it comes from the Spirit, is contagious for some but threatening to many more. The Scriptures testify that the innovator invites trouble. "It is better for one man to die for the people . . . " (Jn. 11:50). Heads shake, hallowed traditions are invoked, non-historical orthodoxy is extolled, and the guilt-tripping begins. Guilt-tripping is a powerful and cruel weapon, especially in the hands of professionals. It beclouds the issue, destroys objectivity and turns discussion into diatribe. Retaliation is the usual response of the immature, and a potentially productive and creative conflict is defeated by mutual defensiveness.

Soon the risk-takers find that they are travelling in bad company. The historical Jesus was no outlaw, and nothing in the gospel lends support to the notion that he was a maverick harboring a grudge against the world, the law or the authorities. Still, his family thought he needed custodial care (Mk. 3:21), the Pharisees suspected a demonic seizure (Mk. 3:22), and bystanders called him some very bad names. Jesus listened to another voice, sought his spiritual direction elsewhere, and seemed unafraid of what people might say about him or what people might do to him.

"Behaviorally, Jesus was perhaps judged unfaithful. He was at odds with the religious understandings faithfully held at the time; he broke laws and traditions when the love of persons demanded it. For Jesus it was more vital to be an honest, genuine human being than a model Jew. Fidelity for Jesus meant a total immersion in life to discover both his humanity and divinity."[9]

Begrudgingly, his enemies were forced to acknowledge his integrity: "We know that you are an honest man, that you are not afraid of anyone, because a man's rank means nothing to you, and that you teach the way of God in all honesty" (M. 12:14). Though a ploy to trap him, this admission tells us something of the impact Jesus had on people. A life of integrity has prophetic clout, even among skeptics and unbelievers. Richard J. Foster has noted that the evangelical impact of the Methodist preacher John Wesley was tremendously enhanced by the integrity of his life. "Wesley is reported to have told his sister, 'Money never stays with me. It would burn me if it did. I throw it out of my hands as soon as possible, lest it should find its way within my heart." He told everyone that, if at his death he had more than ten pounds (about $23) in his possession, people had the privilege of calling him a robber."[10]

Once upon a time in my seminary days, I was wrongly accused of insubordination and forewarned that that not only would my future actions be monitored but that my ordination was in jeopardy. It was a devastating moment. I was frightened and angry, filled with self-pity and confusion. The moment of truth and freedom came when I decided that ordination was not so almighty important, that it was more pleasing to God to be my real self than a model cleric, an honest disciple than an intimidated priest.

In the history of Christian discipleship, this little incident pales into insignificance beside the heroism of the apostles and martyrs; surely it will never be recorded in Butler's lives of the saints. Still, it gave me a taste for the way of integrity and a desire for the serenity of self-acceptance.

The dilemma of Daniel Berrigan and the tragic death of archbishop Oscar Romero give us pause. They alert the Christian community to the dangers of discipleship and the price of integrity. Both men assaulted tradition, the law, the authorities, the past and the establishment. One is in prison and the other is dead. The prophetic style points to the Cross. But it is the cross of Jesus Christ and only the cross that rises as a luminous signpost in the darkness of our world.

Footnotes

1 *Jesus, the Man and the Myth,* James Mackey, Ibid. p. 148.

2 *Looking for Jesus,* Adrian van Kaam. Dimension Books Inc. Denville, N.J. 1978. p. 79.

3 *Jesus, the Way to Freedom,* Donald P. Gray. St. Mary's College Press, Terrace Heights, Winona, Minnesota 55987. p. 47. This little 72-page book is scholarly yet eminently readable. It breathes the air of the gospel and suffuses the light of the Spirit. Gray's vision of Jesus is like refreshing rain falling on parched earth. Highly recommended.

4 *Ibid.* p. 50.

5 Mackey, *Ibid.* p. 265.

6 *Collected Works of C. G. Jung,* translated by R. F. C. Hull. Princeton Univ. Press, Princeton, N.J. 1973. Quoted by Pock, *Ibid.* p. 17.

7 *Intimacy,* Affirmation Books, Whitinsville, MA. 1978. From the essay, "Intimacy with the Self vs. Self-Alienation," Philomena Agudo. p. 18.

8 *The Farther Reaches of Human Nature,* A. H. Maslow, Esalen Books, N.Y. 1975. Quoted by Agudo, *Ibid.* p. 19.

9 *Fidelity,* Affirmation Books, Ibid. Essay by Kathleen E. Kelley, "Never Grow Tired of Doing What is Right". p. 122.

10 *Freedom of Simplicity,* Richard J. Foster. Harper and Row, N.Y. 1981. p. 66.

SEVEN

COMPASSION AND THE CROSS

BEVERLY HILLS, CA. — They call it "The Gold-Paved Gulch," "The Billion Dollar Bazaar," "Rolls Royce Raceway." In recent years Rodeo Drive, a scant three blocks of fashion and high finance, has eclipsed famous shopping streets the world over in status and flamboyant selling style. It is a gathering place for astronomically priced treasures and costly whimsies.

The shops boggle the imagination: a $62,000 automobile sat majestically in the middle of Mr. Guy, an elegant menswear store on the Drive. A $1,600 suede and beaver vest and a $5,500 beaver and suede topcoat were for sale at Bijou. Nearby on a marble display table from Versailles rested a blue gray fox bedspread for $32,000. Customers order two dozen shirts at a time, not just a single replacement. Across the street at Juschi's you could purchase a $950 cotton warm up jacket hand-embroidered in Germany or a knit and suede poncho to toss over jeans at $2,200. Fred's jewelry store offered a bracelet containing two matched gold sapphires, 50 karats each, plus 20-karat diamonds and onyx accents, at a modest $59,000. A mendicant Franciscan on a sight-seeing spree, who desperately needed a haircut, could be accommodated at Jon Peters for $60 . . . .

EL PASO, TX. — Directly across the border is the fifth largest city in Mexico, Juarez, with a population of 750,000. Poverty of body, soul and spirit ravages tens of thousands of these people in desperate want. The Lord's Food Bank was started here in 1975 by Father Rick Thomas S.J., to minister to the needy in the barios and those who literally scavenge scraps from the city *garbage dump.*

Recently a weary, 68-year-old woman named Juanita came for help. For years she had been rummaging through trash at the city market, barely managing to exist herself and attempting to feed her orphaned grandchildren on whatever rotten food she could salvage from garbage cans. She was never able to retrieve enough for all the children to get something to eat. Sometimes they ate once a day; others, they would go without food for days at a time.

On June 23, the water shortage in Juarez became acute. People were roaming the streets with buckets begging for something to drink. The temperature had been over 100 degrees for many days. Babies were dying of dehydration. In the Food Bank area, families receive their water in 55 gallon drums from a passing truck if they have 20¢ to pay. It was shocking and heartbreaking to see people suffering the torture of thirst and babies dying for lack of water . . . .

In any society, secular or sacred, where the haves do not share with the have-nots, the Kingdom of Satan reigns. The presence, the word, the dream of Jesus Christ is neither real nor operative. It simply does not exist.

We Americans make up only five percent of the world's population but each year we consume almost half of the world's production of natural resources. While the poor in under-developed countries consider themselves fortunate to have shacks to shelter them from the weather, we enjoy comparatively lavish luxuries — a summer home, a second automobile, a multi-colored wardrobe. We eat grain-fed beef and annually throw to our pets enough food to feed large segments of the Third World. The population of Juarez could be fed off the garbage from our dumps.

I am not an economist and have neither the academic background, scientific expertise nor political savvy to spearhead a Christian revolution or even speak in an intelligent way to the urgent question of the re-distribution of the world's resources. However, this much can be said without fear of contradiction or polemical exaggeration: "The only sin of Dives (Lk. 17:19-31) seems to have been to live in luxury in the presence of dire need. If the sayings of Jesus do not imply that sharing one's wealth is a duty, they imply nothing."[1]

With the penury of the garbage dump and the luxury of Rodeo Drive in the background, we come to the theme of this final chapter: we re-live the passion of Jesus through a life of compassion.

The etymology or root meaning of compassion stems from the Latin words *cum patior* meaning to suffer with, endure with, struggle with, partake of the hunger, nakedness, loneliness, pain and broken dreams of our brothers and sisters in the human family. Commitment to Jesus Christ without compassion for his people is a lie. "The life of Jesus suggests that godlikeness means to attain a compassionate life since God's heart is apparently thought by Jesus to be compassionate. To show compassion is to be like God, like Abba. To show compassion is to be like Abba's Son."[2]

To listen carefully to his words, "Be compassionate as your heavenly Father is compassionate," is to draw close to the Jesus of the gospels. Matthew's version reads: "You must therefore be perfect as your heavenly Father is perfect" (5:48). As we mentioned earlier, Scripture scholars tell us that the two words can be reduced to the same reality. "Following Jesus in his ministry of compassion defines the meaning of being perfect as your heavenly Father is perfect."[3]

The life of integrity born of fidelity to the dream has a precise meaning in the mind of Christ. It leaves no room for romanticized idealism, condescending pity or sentimental piety. When a disciple's every response, word and decision is motivated by compassion, he has put on Christ and walks in the way of integrity. Biblically, compassion means action. Copious Christian tears for the dehydrated babies in Juarez is heartfelt emotion; when combined with giving them a cup of water it is compassion. The difference between emoting and acting is trenchantly described in the first letter of John: "If a man who was rich enough in this world's goods saw that one of his brothers was in need, but closed his heart to him, how could the love of God be living in him? My children, our love is not to be just words or mere talk, but something real and active" (1 Jn. 3:18).

Every time the gospels mention that Jesus was moved with the deepest emotions or felt sorry for people, it led to his doing something — physical or inner healing, deliverance or exorcism, feeding the hungry crowds or intercessory prayer. The Good Samaritan was commended precisely because he acted. The priest and Levite, paragons of Jewish virtue, flunked the test because they didn't do anything. "Which of these three, in your opinion, was neighbor to the man who fell in with the robbers? The answer came, 'the one who treated him with compassion'. Jesus said to them, 'Then go and do the same'" (Lk. 10:36-37). The unglamorous and little-publicized works of mercy, feeding and sheltering, visiting the sick and incarcerated, educating, correcting, healing words, bearing wrongs, counseling, washing dirty feet and praying with people embody the kingdom lifestyle. So central is this teaching that at the final judgment God himself disappears and is recognizable only in human beings: "I tell you most solemnly, insofar as you did this to one of these least brothers of mine, you did it to me" (Mt. 25:40). "Thus it can be said with certitude that the Biblical meaning of spiritual perfection is to be compassionate."[4]

Of course, the implication here is a very real death to self and to one's own invulnerable stands of rectitude, justice, fair play and fun. Our natural repugnance and ingrained resistance to the inconvenient, unpleasant and often messy business of compassionate caring is well illustrated by a story told at a recent AA meeting: A construction worker stopped after work for a few beers at the local watering hole and got home just in time for dinner. His little daughter, who had peanut butter and jelly all over her face as well as a deposit in her pants, rushed into his arms. To say that he was 'taken aback' would not accurately describe his emotional state. Wheeling around to his wife he muttered, "How the hell do you love something that smells like this?" Calmly she replied, "In the same way I love a husband who comes home stinking drunk and amorous. You work at it."

"Compassion is a spirituality of meat, not milk; of adults, not children; of love, not masochism; of justice, not philanthropy. It requires maturity, a big heart, a willingness to risk and imagination."[5]

Our human experience tells us that Christian marriage is usually not lived to a lyrical beat; it often comes to awkward expression in our fumbling attempts to forgive and make peace, to walk a mile in the other's mocassins, and to share the frightened, lonely, insecure and sometimes neurotic journey of our spouse through the way of compassion. We can find echoes of ourselves in the petty, strange and broken syllables of their story. With remarkable insight Vincent DePaul wrote: "Be compassionate and you will become a saint."

However in the contemporary church there is sufficient experience of failed human situations which make continued co-habitation intolerable if not impossible. Diocesan marriage tribunals are surfeited with annulment requests. Their overcrowded dockets frequently prevent immediate redress especially in densely populated urban areas. In the past ten years the number of annulments granted in the American Catholic Church has spiralled at a 500 percent ratio. These statistics do not warrant conclusions of laxity and lunatic liberalism in canonical jurisprudence but to the humble acknowledgment that, due to spiritual immaturity and inadequate preparation, many of the sacramental marriages celebrated in the past were neither sacraments nor celebrations. The love of Christ for the Church, re-actualized in every Christian marriage, is simply non-existent when either one or both spouses do not know Jesus. The crisis in the church is a crisis of faith, the need to know Jesus

Christ as saving Lord, and married couples are knee deep in the throes of the crisis.

The teaching of Jesus on the indissolubility of marriage (Mk. 10:1-12, Mt. 5:31-32, Mt. 19:3-12, Lk. 16:18) is unbending and rigorous without qualification. This conclusion must be taken for granted. Divorce is an evil and the cause of irreparable harm. Any attempt to mitigate the truth of this teaching would plunge the church into the moral morass of divorce on demand. Yet, the absolute, total and unequivocal prohibition of divorce often makes it impossible to show compassion. St. Paul did not hesitate to intervene in the case of a believer married to a non-believer. Invoking his own apostolic authority, he modified the teaching of Jesus and dissolved the marriage because "God has called us to a life of peace" (1 Co. 7:15). Thus the so-called Pauline privilege was introduced into the life of the Church and later incorporated into its code of canon law.

The Church, the visible extension of Jesus Christ in time and space, is the image of the Compassionate One. Without diluting the gospel or abrogating tradition, we must not beg the question, "What would the Master do?," with a failed human situation that is unilaterally or mutually destructive and injurious to the lives of others. Fr. John McKenzie writes: "If the problem of divorce had been treated by the kind of reasoning which gave us the morality of legitimate self-defense and the just war, we should long ago have found the legitimate and just divorce. We have found ways to avoid the teaching of Jesus on violence which is as clear as his teaching on divorce. Apparently we see an 'intrinsic evil' in sexual intercourse which we do not see in killing."[6]

Compassion is not sloppy sentimentality nor does it comprise the truth. Any spirituality that tampers with the Word of God from naive humanitarian motives is bankrupt. St. Augustine observed long ago that, where there is any scent of a lie, the authority of the truth is immediately weakened. Biblical compassion, combining heartfelt emotion with active relief for the suffering, transcends psychological personalism and privatized pity, to enter into the very heart and mystery of God. Clear-minded, hard-headed and soft-hearted, Jesus revealed in his ministry of mercy the face of the compassionate God. Pursuing McKenzie's thought on divorce: "The Christian should be able to find a position between inhumane rigidity and amoral relaxation. Jesus certainly stated without qualification the principle that marriage is a stable and total commitment. Nothing is gained by viewing marriage as anything else. If it is a temporary sexual encounter it cannot be an element in a stable society. Jesus taught this: did he also teach that there is no recovery from mistakes, especially if they be the mistakes of others or the mistakes of adolescence? One needs clearer evidence than has been adduced that this is really the teaching of Jesus. There are irreparable sins and errors, like murder; one hopes that these can be kept to a minimum without encouraging them."[7]

The compassion of Jesus should motivate us to re-examine the personal response we make and the pastoral wisdom we proffer when confronted with a wedding invitation that does not fulfill all the canonical requirements for validity and liceity; it should further encourage us to assume the burden of moral responsibility for decisions and life situations which the Master did not prefabricate for us. An evangelical rule of thumb: Jesus seemed to have been less distressed by faux pas born of benevolence than by errors rising from legalism.

Last winter I spent ten days at Fr. Bruce Ritter's Covenant House in New York City. The community residence is located on 8th Avenue between 43rd and 44th Streets. The community is tightly-knit, the life of prayer real and rhythmic, the ministry to runaway children, teen-age prostitutes and chemically de-pendent youth exhausting and deeply evangelical. Late one afternoon I sauntered over to the Times Square area. When I saw a musclebound pimp screaming filth at one of the girls in his stable, I pretended not to notice. Ahead, the movie marquee blinked "kiddie porn" and cautioned the fainthearted not to venture inside. On the corner, two Hispanic hookers in their mid-twenties were soliciting unwary customers. I retreated into a doorway and proceeded to pass through several shades of the emotional spectrum — from a wave of revolt and disgust to anger and frustration and finally to sadness, empti-ness and pain.

The compassionate love of Jesus Christ is another matter entirely. His compassion surges from the bowels of his being, reveals a depth that defies human understanding and operates on a level that escapes human imitation. The numerous physical healings performed by Jesus to alleviate human misery are only a hint of the anguish in the heart of God's Son for suffering humanity. Here the disciple and the seeker after truth kneel in the presence of Mystery.

"The English word for 'compassion' is far too weak to express the emotion that moved Jesus. The Greek verb *splagchnizomai* used in all these texts is derived from the noun *splagchnon,* which means intestines, bowels, entrails or heart, that is to say, the inward parts from which strong emotions seem to arise. The Greek verb therefore means a movement or impulse that wells up from one's very entrails, a gut reaction. That is why English translations have to resort to expressions like 'he was *moved* with compassion or pity' (AV, RV, JB) or he *felt* sorry (JB) or 'his *heart* went out to them' (NEB). But even these do not capture the deep physical and emotional flavour of the Greek word for compassion. That Jesus was moved by some such emotion is beyond all reasonable doubt."[8]

The Christ who weeps over Times Square is the man of sorrows moved in the pit of his stomach for the lostness of the sheep who do not know him. The heart of the crucified Lord of Glory does not turn away in revulsion or disgust at the wretchedness and perversity of the human condition. There is no crime so horrible or no sin so despicable that it was left at the foot of the cross. "He took our sickness away and carried our diseases for us." How is this possible?

Because Jesus is God.

He is the incarnation of the compassion of the Father. Meister Eckhart, a 15th century mystic wrote, "You may call God love; you may call God goodness; but the best name for God is Compassion." What do the exalted names — Son of God, Second Person of the Blessed Trinity, Kyrios, Pantocrator and other Christological titles bestowed on Jesus by a later age — signify but that God was present in the Compassionate One in a unique, extravagant and definitive way? Through meal sharing, story-telling, miraculous healing, preaching, teaching and a life of compassion which knew no frontiers, boundaries or sectarian divisions, Jesus inaugurated in his person the reign of God. In Jesus' own conduct the new age dawned, the messianic era erupted into history. His disciples' loving concern, non-judgmental attitude and compassionate care for their brothers and sisters is the visible form in which the reign of God is manifested today. What makes the Kingdom come is heartfelt compassion. It is the way that God's lordship takes.

The ministry of the church to the lost sheet of Times Square, the deprived at the Dump, the habitues of Rodeo Drive and every affluent nook and impoverished cranny of the glove where the Compassionate One is not known, is not motivated by a desire for novelty. It is a compulsion of love. "If we do not commit ourselves with urgency to the task of evangelization, we are guilty of an inexcusable lack of compassion."[9]

The church and the bible are not substitutes for God but means through which man makes conscious contact with Jesus Christ. They are the place of encounter with the Compassionate One who reveals himself in sundry ways and diverse temperaments. The sinfulness and vulnerability of the disciples are no stumbling block because "his power is at its best in weakness" (2 Co. 12:9).

What is indeed crucial to the evangelical enterprise is the awareness that we ourselves are the primary target. It is not 'they' who are poor, sinful and lost. It is ourselves. Unless we acknowledge that we are the sinners, the sick ones and the lost sheep for whom Jesus came, we do not belong to the 'blessed' who know that they are poor and inherit the kingdom. Enough of our pseudo-messianic posturing! Let us be done with our futile attempts to appear righteous before God! The Amen, the faithful, the true Witness says: "I know all about you: you are neither cold nor hot. I wish you were one or the other, but since you are neither, but only lukewarm, I will spit you out of my mouth. You say to yourself, 'I am rich, I have made a fortune, and have everything I want,' never realizing that you are wretchedly and pitiably poor, and blind and naked too" (Rv. 3:15-17).

In returning to ourselves, in contemplating the compassion of Jesus and realizing that 'this means me,' we come under the Mercy and qualify for the name-tag 'blessed.' In urging us to compassionate caring for others, Jesus invites us to have compassion for ourselves. The measure of our compassion for others lies in proportion to our capacity for self-acceptance and self-affirmation. When the compassion of Christ is interiorized and appropriated to self, the breakthrough into being for others occurs. In a catch-22 situation, the way of compassionate caring for others brings healing to ourselves, and compassionate caring for ourselves brings healing to others. Solidarity with human suffering frees the one who receives and liberates the one who gives through the conscious awareness "I am the other."

Self-hatred stands as an insuperable obstacle to growth and maturity. It derails interaction with others and renders us impotent to give or receive love. The memory selects only negative recollections. Previous kindnesses and thoughtful gestures are perceived as vitiated by self-seeking. All other emotions are blocked out. A sense of personal worthlessness prevails. We become more closed, less communicative, more uncomfortable to be around. If prevailed upon to speak, we express deep disappointment at our lack of spiritual progress and dwell on the unlikelihood of future improvement. Caring for others is existentially impossible because we cannot be compassionate toward ourselves.

The thesis of this book is not gratuitous guesswork. Psychologists and psychiatrists, counselors and confessors live in the real world and devote an enormous amount of time/talent to people who dislike themselves. Years ago Carl Jung wrote:

> The acceptance of oneself is the essence of the whole moral problem and the epitome of a whole outlook on life. That I feed the hungry, that I forgive an insult, that I love my enemy in the name of Christ — all these are undoubtedly great virtues. What I do unto the least of my brethren, that I do unto Christ. But what if I should discover that the least amongst them all, the poorest of all the beggars, the most impudent of all the offenders, the very enemy himself — that these are within me, and that I myself stand in need of the alms of my own kindness — that I myself am the enemy who must be loved — what then? As a rule, the Christian's attitude is then reversed; there is no longer any question of love or long-suffering; we say to the brother within us 'Raca,' and condemn and rage against ourselves. We hide it from the world; we refuse to admit ever having met this least among the lowly in ourselves."[10]

Who will rewrite the script for self-hatred? The Compassionate One! With a graciousness, a kindness and an understanding of human weakness that only God could inhabit and exhibit, he liberates us from alienation and self-condemnation and offers a new possibility to each of us in our brokenness. He is the Savior who saves us from ourselves. His gospel is Good News: Burn the old tapes spinning round in your head that bind you up and lock you into a self-centered stereotype. Listen to the new song of salvation written for those who know that they are poor. Let go of your fear of my Father and your dislike for yourself. The Knight of the Mirrors lied to Don Quixote when he told him: "See yourself as you really are. Discover that you are not a noble knight, but an idiotic scarecrow of a man." And the Enchanter lies to you when he says: "Thou art no knight but a foolish pretender. Look in the mirror of reality. Behold things are they really are. What dost thou see? Naught but an aging fool." The Father of Lies twists the truth and distorts reality. He is the author of cynicism and skepticism, mistrust and despair, sick thinking and self-hatred. I am the Son of Compassion. You belong to me, and no one will tear you from my hand.

Donald Gray writes: "His compassion enables us to be compassionate toward ourselves. It is the divine compassion that Jesus embodies in human history and in his own compassionate life and death. Before I am asked to show compassion toward my brothers and sisters in their suffering, I am asked to accept the Father's compassion in my own life, to be transformed by it, to become caring and compassionate toward myself in my own suffering and hurt, in my own failure and need. The Father's loving graciousness is not in any way conditioned by or dependent upon what we are or do. He will be gracious and compassionate toward us no matter what we are or do. He will be gracious and compassionate toward us because that is the kind of Father he is — Abba. We should never speak of losing the state of grace in this sense, for God never stops being gracious and faithful to us. His being gracious does not depend on us — he will be unfailingly loving."[11]

We re-live the passion of Jesus through a life of compassion. On the cross the open arms of the Crucified reached out to feel the pain and suffering of the world. The Son of Compassion wanted to absorb the guilt, rejection, shame and failure of his brothers and sisters. He came to us not with the crushing impact of unbearable glory but in the way of weakness, vulnerability and need. Jesus was a naked, humiliated, exposed God on the cross who allowed us to get close to him.

Life teaches us how difficult it is to receive anything from someone who has all the answers, who is completely cool, utterly unafraid, invulnerable, needing nothing and no one, always on top of life and in control of every situation. We feel unnecessary, unneeded and reluctant to receive. So Jesus comes in the way of weakness giving us the chance to love him and making us feel that we have something to give him. Isaiah prophesied that he would be "like a lamb led to slaughter or a sheep before his shearers" (53:7). Jesus, who understands the human heart, allowed the image of a dumb, helpless animal to be applied to himself.

The world does not understand vulnerability. Strength is made to look like weakness and freedom is made to look like failure. Vulnerability is flatly rejected as incompetence and compassionate caring is dismissed as unprofitable. The great deception of commercial television advertising is that being poor, vulnerable and weak is uncool and ineffectual. A fat monk named 'Brother Dominic' is cute and cool because he buys into the competitive game of a copy machine. Social climbing, power and winning breed a spirit of competition that bids farewell to compassion. The spirituality of the Servant is simply incomprehensible to the advertising industry. "The opening notes of Beethoven's Fifth Symphony are being employed to sell us pain reliever and the Prayer of St. Francis is being used to sell us hair conditioner."[12]

The cross of Jesus will ever remain a scandal and foolishness to discriminating disciples who seek a triumphal savior and a prosperity gospel. Their number is legion. They are enemies of the cross of Christ. Jesus would have no other name by which he could be called were it not the name of the crucified. "He is unmistakable and identifiable only as the man of the cross."[13] His ministry was a seeming failure, his life appeared to have made no difference; he was a naked, murdered, ineffectual, losing God. But in that weakness and vulnerability, the world would come to know the love of the Abba of the Compassionate One.

Rosemary Haughton writes: "The paradox of passion is that the thrust of love seeking love consists in being vulnerable ... There is no dignity or shame in the naked suffering of the passion of Jesus. There is only utter vulnerability, a giving which is so absolute that Christian imagination has all too often been at work to mitigate the horror, either by supposing that the Son of God had evacuated the condemned body of Jesus at some point sufficiently beforehand to leave scope for majesty, or simply by sentimentalizing the thing into a kind of divine heroism. It is not heroism. It is simply love."[14]

The glory of Jesus lies in this: in weakness, vulnerability and apparent failure he has called forth disciples to come after him, willing and able to carry the cross and re-live his passion through a life of compassion. They are marginal people, not part of the scene, irrelevant to the 'action.' In their ministry of quiet presence they do not need to win or compete. They may look like losers even to themselves. The world ignores them. But they are building the Kingdom of God on earth by reaching out in vulnerability and weakness to share the suffering of their brothers and sisters. Where the Compassionate One is, there will his servants be. Whether in Times Square, Juarez, Rodeo Drive, middle class suburbia, an alcoholic rehabilitation center or a roomful of eighth graders, the Word stands: "I assure you, as often as you did it for one of my least brothers, you did it for me." The life of integrity finds its foundation and criterion in the cross, right down to everyday life; and the passion of Jesus Christ is re-lived through compassion, right down to the nitty-gritty of everyday life.

Footnotes

¹ McKenzie. *Ibid.* p. 252.

² Gray. *Ibid.* p. 70.

³ Senior. *Ibid.* p. 105.

⁴ *A Spirituality Named Compassion, and the Healing of the Global Village, Humpty Dumpty and Us,* Matthew Fox. Winston Press, Inc., 430 Oak Grove, Minneapolis, Minnesota 55403. 1979. p. 32.

⁵ *Ibid.* p. 17.

⁶ McKenzie. *Ibid.* p. 157.

⁷ *"Jesus and Divorce,"* John L. McKenzie, *Commonweal Magazine,* May 23, 1980. p. 305.

⁸ Nolan. *Ibid.* p. 28.

⁹ "The Thailand Statement," *World Evangelization,* Information Bulletin No. 20, a publication of the Lausanne Committee for World Evangelization, September, 1980. p. 6. Quoted by Foster. *Ibid.* p. 167.

¹⁰ *Modern Man In Search of a Soul,* C. J. Jung. Harcourt, Brace and World Harvest Books, 1933, p. 235. Quoted by Gray, *Ibid.* p. 41.

¹¹ Gray. *Ibid.* p. 41.

¹² Fox. *Ibid.* p. 209.

¹³ *Perspectives on Paul,* Kasemann. *Ibid.* p. 56.

¹⁴ *The Passionate God,* Rosemary Haughton. Paulist Press, 545 Island Road, Ramsey, N.J. 07446. 1981. p. 149.

AFTERWORD

In the place to which the Lord has led me, it would be untimely and inappropriate to write mincing pastorals, sensitive soul blubber or well-behaved meditations for pious people. In this little book I have given my heart and my language license to be what it is: crude and soft-spoken, whole and stricken, honest and provocative, drawn from the casks of life.

On the day that I began the manuscript a friend advised: "Write your book as if you were going to die the day it is published." A melodramatic flourish, perhaps, but in the gathering mist of midlife I am struck by the lateness of the hour, the paramount importance of truth-telling and the urgency of personal integrity.

Within these pages is a glimpse of the Jesus of my life — dreamer and storyteller, parable of the Father, servant, friend, savior and stranger to self-hatred. He calls me back home to himself and myself. Jesus is God to me, not because of the exalted titles bestowed on him by later ages, but because he is the Compassionate One. Compassionate not because he is Son of God but Son of God because he is compassionate in a way that escapes human comprehension or possibility.

Should you choose to call him Goodness he will be good to you; should you choose to call him Love he will be loving to you; should you choose to call him Compassion he will know that you know.